T0316854

THE
PROGRESS OF CAPITALISM
IN ENGLAND

THE
PROGRESS OF CAPITALISM
IN ENGLAND

BY

W. CUNNINGHAM, D.D., F.B.A.

Cambridge:
at the University Press
1925

CAMBRIDGE
UNIVERSITY PRESS

University Printing House, Cambridge CB2 8BS, United Kingdom

Cambridge University Press is part of the University of Cambridge.

It furthers the University's mission by disseminating knowledge in the pursuit of education, learning and research at the highest international levels of excellence.

www.cambridge.org
Information on this title: www.cambridge.org/9781107456372

© Cambridge University Press 1916

First edition 1916
First published 1916
Reprinted 1925
First paperback edition 2014

A catalogue record for this publication is available from the British Library

ISBN 978-1-107-45637-2 Paperback

TO THE

Hon. W. PEMBER REEVES

DIRECTOR OF THE LONDON SCHOOL OF
ECONOMICS AND POLITICS
AND TO MY COLLEAGUES ON THE STAFF

PREFACE

THE following pages contain the substance of Lectures which were delivered in the London School of Economics and Political Science in the spring of 1915. The School is organised with the view of promoting the study of present day problems, such as the actual economic conditions under which the industry and commerce of our own country are carried on, as well as those of the great overseas dominions in which we exert an influence—and of our rivals in trade. There is besides a department of History, which has done a great deal to encourage investigation and research; and this is in itself evidence of recognition of the truth that the present is deeply rooted in the past, and that the anomalies and controversies of the present day only become intelligible when we understand their genesis. These lectures were intended to illustrate the method of treating Economic History which may best meet the requirements of those who are less interested in the economic interpretation of political changes in the past than in obtaining a clear insight into the conditions of the present. It is important to arrange the facts so that the bearing of the past on the present may be easily apprehended and fully appreciated.

The substance of these Lectures is now published in the hope that it may prove a useful appendix to my *Growth of English Industry and Commerce.* Political divisions supply the framework of that book; and though the subject may be conveniently approached from the political side, we do not reach the main object of Economic History if we are content to study it as subsidiary to the Body Politic. The economic activities of every kind which are co-ordinated for the material prosperity of the community—the Body Economic—have grown in efficiency and complexity through all the ages, and under many different forms of political constitution. The stages of development, and the various economic organisms which have succeeded one another, are worth studying systematically and apart from politics altogether; and it is possible to accentuate this economic aspect and mark the steps by which Capitalism has come into being in England. We may come to realise that the study of Economic History gives invaluable help in applying the experience of the past to the solution of the problems of the present day, in every part of the Empire. Due appreciation of the importance of the Body Economic is essential to the wise organisation of the Body Politic.

W. C.

Trinity College, Cambridge,
Michaelmas, 1916.

CONTENTS

PAGE

Contents

I. ECONOMIC HISTORY AND EMPIRICAL ECONOMIC SCIENCE

(1) Both economists and historians have drawn occasionally upon Economic History, but neither have considered it as more than subsidiary to the work in which they were specially interested, or recognised its importance adequately.

From its earliest inception Political Economy has welcomed Economic History in the capacity of a handmaid. Economics has been generally regarded as an empirical science, and economists have been ready to draw on the recorded experience of the past, though their main reliance has naturally been on contemporary evidence. As McCulloch says, "the economist will not arrive at anything like a true knowledge of the laws regulating the production, accumulation, distribution and the consumption of wealth if he do not draw his materials from a very wide surface. He should study man in every situation ; he should have recourse to the history of society, arts, commerce and civilisation, to the works of legislators, philosophers and travellers, to everything in

short that can throw light on the causes which ac-
celerate or retard the progress of nations; he should
mark the changes which have taken place in the
fortunes and conditions of the human race in different
regions and ages of the world; he should trace the
rise, progress and decline of industry, and above all
he should carefully analyse and compare the effects of
different institutions and regulations and discriminate
the various circumstances wherein an advancing and
declining society differ from each other[1]."

Adam Smith's *Wealth of Nations* shows that his
mind was saturated with history; and the eighteenth
century writers on particular branches of Economics
contributed substantial treatises such as Eden's
State of the Poor, and Anderson's *Commerce*, which
show how much they drew on the phenomena of the
distant past in their efforts to understand the conditions of the present.   Malthus' *Essay on Population*
contains a mass of information drawn from many
places and ages, and Richard Jones, his successor at
Haileybury, insisted that it was only by an inductive
method that we could understand the nature of rent as
actually paid[2].   The historical investigations of Tooke
and Thorold Rogers, were specially directed to the

---

[1] McCulloch, *Principles*, p. 21.

[2] *An Essay on the Distribution of Wealth and on the Sources
of Taxation*, 1831.

history of prices. Fleetwood's essay[1] on this subject
had been concerned with a modern problem and the interpretation of a statutory limitation in regard to the
value of a benefice, but in the hands of later investi-
gators the main interest seemed to lie in elucidating
the conditions of bygone days, and getting clearer
light on the habits and resources of men who lived
in the distant past. Prof. Thorold Rogers[2] was
specially taken up with the economic interpretation
of Political History, and does not seem to have
regarded the economic development of the country
as itself deserving of systematic study.

Historians in the nineteenth century were, like the
early economists, very ready to welcome the fresh
light which might be drawn from Economic History.
The stately writers, who regarded economic detail as
unworthy of the dignity of History, were no longer
dominant. Special chapters, which gave the essential
setting of political events were commonly introduced;
and popular writers were frankly jealous of the stress
which had been laid on Military and Political History,
and were anxious that the "real life of the people," in
its economic as well as in its other aspects, should be
a subject of study; but the ordinary reader finds

[1] *Chronicon Preciosum*, 1745.
[2] The importance for economic studies of the investigation of relative prices in the present and in the past is brought
out by Prof. Nicholson, *Principles*, III. 65.

more interest in the delineation of character and the explanation of policy, than in the recounting of schemes for the development of national resources.

There were also those who dwelt on the unity of History and who recognised that primitive man, in all places and times, had similar problems to face in his struggles with nature, and that there were interesting analogies in the different methods that had been adopted by different races for engaging in this struggle. Sir Henry Maine called attention to the *Village Community* as a wide-spread institution; and much interest has been found in noting how other races are passing through experiences that we have ourselves outlived. From these causes Economic History has been generally regarded as having closer affinities with History than with Economics, and it has been developed in directions which seemed to be more concerned with the pedantries of the past than with the problems of the present.

(2) This less friendly attitude has been specially adopted by those writers who regard Political Economy not as an empirical science, but as a branch of Social Philosophy[1]. The introduction of this habit of thought

[1] For a general criticism of the Social Philosophy which modern Political Economy takes for granted see J. Hutchison Stirling, *Secret of Hegel*, II. 541 f.   For a brief criticism of its most recent form, see my *Christianity and Economic Science*, p. 90.

was partly due to religious teachers; they felt that
the principles according to which society was governed
were the principles of Divine government. Thus
President Weyland regarded science as "a systematic
arrangement of the laws which God has established
in so far as they have been discovered in any department of human knowledge. It is obvious on the
slightest reflection that the Creator has subjected the
accumulations of the blessings of this life to some
determinate laws....Political Economy therefore, is
a systematic arrangement of the laws by which under
our present constitution the relations of man, whether
individual or social, to the objects of his desire, are
governed[1]." A somewhat similar view was taken
by Dr Chalmers, who found "a counterpoise to the
laws of Nature in what may be termed the laws of
Political Economy[2]."

An impulse of a similar kind was given by the
religion of Humanity, and the Social Philosophy of
Comte. The influence of his writings may be traced
in chapter after chapter of Mill's *Principles*; and
though Mill continued to treat Political Economy as
an empirical science[3], he was conscious of the claims

[1] *Elements of Political Economy* (1837), p. 3.

[2] Chalmers, *Christian and Civic Economy of large Towns*
(1821), III. 38.

[3] In his treatment of cottiers and metayers Mill was
apparently influenced by Richard Jones, the great advocate
of empirical study.

of the new philosophy to constant consideration, and entitled his book *Principles of Political Economy with some of their Applications to Social Philosophy.* Economists appeared to popular apprehension[1] to lay undue stress on external conditions, and they certainly gave great prominence to the generalisations of empirical science. It was indeed recognised that the laws of distribution were really dependent on the changing conditions of society, but the principles of production appeared to have all the cogency of laws of the physical order. Economic laws came to be spoken of as formulating what is generally true in society, and as stating what becomes increasingly true as civilisation advances. As this habit of mind obtained a firmer and firmer hold, historical enquiries seemed to be of less importance: if Social Philosophy laid down laws which were universally true, the investigation of phenomena that could not readily be reduced to the realm of law was superfluous, and History was only worth referring to for the sake of illustrations of the principles which Social Philosophy had established[2].

[1] See p. 113 below.

[2] The students of Economic History in the eighties were not content with the limited rôle which was thus assigned them. It is seldom worth while to go back on forgotten controversies, but the articles on "A Plea for Pure Theory" in the *Economic Review* (1892), and on the "Perversion of

(3) This new departure in treating Political Economy as a branch of Social Philosophy was not merely antagonistic to the empirical study of the phenomena of the past, but has resulted in the entire re-casting of Political Economy as it had been hitherto understood. The subject matter of the science or art had been habitually confined to external phenomena that could be observed, and by reference to which our generalisations could be tested. Economics, as now re-cast, took internal conditions of motive and satisfaction as its subject matter; and the leading conceptions of the old economic writers were also modified. Economics could no longer be charged with ignoring human nature altogether, though there was no sufficient recognition of the varieties and the changes in human nature. Instead of regarding the conditions of Exchange as the main consideration, the new economists devoted themselves to an analysis of Utility; and while they gained some advantage in this new mode of statement and in the simplification of certain problems, they shifted the basis on which

Economic History," *Economic Journal* (1892), and *Academy* (Oct. 1, 1892), had an effect in securing freedom for economic research in connection with the Historical School at Cambridge. Since that date there has been no attempt to insist that the teaching of Economic History shall be governed by the desire to illustrate economic laws.

the truth of economic principles had hitherto rested. Such an attempted revolution was not allowed to pass unquestioned; it had been already admitted[1] that economic doctrines, as stated by Ricardo, disregarded ordinary phraseology and had little to do with ordinary life, and social philosophers failed to recognise that this was a defect.   The protest in favour of empirical study was waived aside by those who were treating Political Economy as a branch of Social Philosophy, as a mere whim of men like Schmoller and an advanced German School, which were "arrogant and exclusive in their pretensions[2]."   But it might have been expected that English economists should at least take account of the criticisms which had been pronounced by anticipation, by one of the pioneers in

[1] McCulloch was probably the author of the critique on Jones's *Distribution of Wealth*, in which his objections to Ricardo are dismissed on the following grounds.   "It will be sufficient to observe here that Mr Ricardo's book is one of principle only, and that it is not to be judged of by a merely practical standard....He was as well aware as Mr Jones or any one else that the rent, the origin and progress of which he had undertaken to investigate, was not what is commonly called rent."   *Edinburgh Review*, LIV. 85.

[2] Keynes, *Scope and Method*, p. 26.   This appreciation of Schmoller personally does not appear to be either well-informed or judicial.   In any case a criticism is not necessarily to be ignored because of the eccentricities or unimportance of the persons by whom the criticism has been urged.   Dr Marshall, *Economic Journal* (II. 508), 1892, and Prof. Pigou, *Morning Post*, 1 and 3 May, 1916, seem to have fallen into this mistake.

presenting in a mathematical form the doctrines which had been generally accepted as part of the science of Political Economy. Whewell's first endeavours in this direction date as far back as 1829; he said, "I am aware that many may at first regard this endeavour as necessarily barren of any practical and rational results. And this opinion would be undoubtedly true if it were intended to make mathematical calculations supply the place of moral reasoning; or if it were maintained that we could by the use of algebraical symbols obtain any results of a nature different to those which we can obtain otherwise. It is not, however, with any such views that I now enter upon the subject. But I hope in the course of the following pages to make it appear that some parts of this science of Political Economy may be presented in a more systematic and connected form and, I would add, more simply and clearly by the use of mathematical language than without such help." " For my own part, I do not conceive that we are at all justified in asserting the principles which form the basis of Mr Ricardo's system, either to be steady and universal in their operation, or to be of such paramount and predominant influence, that that and other principles, which control and oppose them, may be neglected in comparison. Some of them appear to be absolutely false in general, and others to be inapplicable in almost all particular cases[1]." Twenty years later he wrote, "It would, however, be to take a very erroneous view of the consequences of this application of mathematics to Political Economy, to suppose that it can add anything to the certainty of the fundamental principles. There is perhaps in some persons a propensity to believe that any subject, when clothed in a mathematical shape, acquires something of mathematical demonstrative character; and that by applying mathematics to assumed principles of knowledge, we in some measure create a science. I must beg leave very distinctly to repudiate all pretensions of this kind. By stating distinctly our fundamental principles, which such an undertaking as the present requires us to do, we may bring them more clearly under notice and examination than would otherwise be done; but we add nothing whatever to the evidence of the principles...[2]."

"Mathematics," he insists, "is the logic of quantity, and will necessarily, sooner or later, become the instrument of all sciences where quantity is the subject treated and deductive reasoning the process employed. I am, however, well aware, that the pretensions of Political Economy to such a

[1] Papers before the *Cambridge Philosophical Society*, March 2, 1829, p. 2, and April 18, 1831, p. 2.

[2] *Ibid*. April 15, 1850.

scientific character, are as yet entirely incapable of being supported. Any attempt to make this subject at present a branch of Mathematics, could only lead to a neglect or perversion of facts, and to a course of trifling speculations, barren distinctions and useless logomachies[1]." Whewell was perfectly clear as to the empirical character of the truth of economic principles, and seems to go as far as Schmoller in his suspicions of the treatment of Political Economy as a branch of Social Philosophy which rests not on observations but on principles which are spoken of as if they had authority on religious or ethical grounds, and had a superior certainty to merely empirical generalisations about wealth.

As Whewell had died in 1866 it was simpler for writers in the eighties to ignore him than it would have been to reply to him, but those who have followed him in the mathematical treatment of economic doctrines have not been wise in discarding his warning. Principles which do not rest on a basis of observed fact, are neither to be trusted as giving us accurate knowledge of phenomena nor can we rely on them for practical guidance. As Prof. Edgeworth puts it, "most of the abstract truths of Political Economy are to be regarded only as first approximations to be supplemented in practice by concrete circumstances[2]";

[1] *Ibid*. April 18, 1831. p. 43.   [2] *Economic Journal*, XXVI. 225.

Economic History is just the study of these concrete circumstances, and of the genesis of existing conditions. In order to deal with actual problems in all their complexity we must take account of special conditions in place and time. If Political Economy is treated as a branch of Social Philosophy, it ceases to have to do with external phenomena and becomes instead a doctrine as to the workings of the modern mind, and the play of various subjective motives which do not lend themselves to accurate observation or to careful verification. Statements regarding the working of the modern mind may be very general in form and apply to the inhabitants of Saturn, if their minds are similar to that of the nineteenth century Englishman. But we have no right to assume that we have, in this country or in this decade, attained the final development, either of society or of the individual. Indeed, though the nineteenth century mind survives among us still, there is some reason for thinking that the Social Philosophy of the eighties and nineties is already an anachronism. Social philosophers are in danger of trying to adjust new facts to the old formulae, they have been able to give little light in regard to the problems presented by the war, since they regard it as a mere aberration in which the laws of Political Economy have ceased to apply. The facts of life are very complex, and there

is need of a cultivated judgment in order to discern
the main issue in the circumstances of any particular
case. Great problems have been raised by the material
waste which is due to the war, and as to the sudden
readjustment which will be needed when the war[1]
is over. To regard the main question as one of
taxation and of the right application of Adam
Smith's principle of equality is an inadequate way
of treating the cost of the war. The theory of taxation is important; but it does not give the means of
discussing the wisest course for the country to adopt
with regard to the recovery of the country after the
war. "The worst use of theory," as Lord Acton said,
"is to make men insensible to fact[2]." The logical
objections to regarding Political Economy as a branch
of Social Philosophy have been reinforced, so far as
the public mind is concerned, by its inability to give
guidance on present day affairs. The professors[3] who
protested that there could be no change of circum-
stance which made it desirable to re-consider the
trading policy of this country, did much to discredit
the scientific character of the doctrine they taught; a
mode of treatment that is neither fruitful in research
nor reliable in practical affairs has little to be said for

---

[1] Compare my paper on economic problems after the war
in Prof. C. Kirkaldy's *Industrial Credit of the War*, Chapter v.

[2] *English Historical Review*, 1. 40.

[3] *Times*, 15 Aug. 1903.

it; and "consumers' rent" and "immaterial capital" may soon be relegated to the Limbo to which planetary influences and the signatures of plants have long since been consigned by the progress of empirical science.

(4) During the later half of the nineteenth century the study of Economic History has received a new impulse since it has come to be gradually recognised that a knowledge of historical conditions is not an idle pedantry, but is essential for the understanding of present day problems; and that it is desirable to draw on human experience of every kind in attempting to deal with the complexities of modern life. Richard Jones insisted that the economic development of England was much in advance of that of other countries[1], and that it was an error to treat the principles, which held good in the special circumstances of England, as true for the world as a whole. His *Political Economy of Nations*[2] fell rather flat in his own country; but a similar point of view[3] was adopted by several German writers who set themselves to investigate the reasons why England

[1] *Literary Remains*, edited by Whewell, p. 558.

[2] *Ibid.* 337.

[3] There does not seem to be any direct evidence of dependence; but as List was in Europe in the early thirties, and was making a special study of English economic conditions, it is not likely that he was wholly unaware of Richard Jones's books and teaching.

had attained such remarkable industrial success. List's *National System of Political Economy* led practical men to consider the methods by which English industrial greatness had been built up in the eighteenth century, and pointed out the possibilities of out-rivalling her successfully. Roscher[1] made a careful study of the early literature of Economics in England, and Brentano's essay on *Guilds and Trades Unions*[2] made it clear that it is worth while to take History into account with regard to social institutions, as in considering political schemes. These German writers reacted on English opinion and gradually the importance of going back to even more remote times was recognised. According to his son, Mr Seebohm's "historical works were the result of the need he felt to search into the past for a clue to the present environment in which he found himself and in which he was living so full and active a life[3]." The *English Village Community* was not merely a remarkable work in itself but it gave an extraordinary impulse to a new generation to devote themselves to historical investigation for the sake of its bearing on present day issues. To Arnold Toynbee and those who came

---

[1] *Zur Geschichte der englischen Volkswirtschaftslehre* in *Abhandlungen der phil.-hist. Classe der k. sachs. Gesell. d. Wissen.* II. Leipzig, 1857.

[2] *Die Arbeitergilden der Gegenwart* (1871).

[3] Preface to the *Spirit of Christianity*, by F. Seebohm, p. vi.

under his influence, history was a living thing which
could not be relegated to the background by the
student of social phenomena; in an old country the
experience of the past has been recognised in recent
times as an essential element in economic study.

(5) While social philosophers have busied themselves with elaborating cosmopolitan theories, there
has been continued and increasing activity in the
careful study of the economic condition of our own
country, and of the oversea dominions.   The economic
investigations undertaken on behalf of government
have been of special interest. A large number of
commissions have been appointed and their reports
contain masses of observed facts in regard to
modern times; the records of survivals in particular
districts, like the Report of the Crofters' Commission
and Prof. Scott's Report on the Industries of the
Highlands and Islands, are of special interest, as well
as the surveys by the Government of India of the
economic progress which is made from decade to
decade.   There has been a great advance of empirical
economic science, in the collecting of data; and these
are so complicated that it is necessary to simplify
the problems by abstraction and generalisation; and
this process, when verification is possible, enables us to
state what is true for limited periods and areas. For

forecasting the future, it is necessary to put forward some hypothesis and deduce from it what is likely to occur in certain assumed conditions; but even when the conclusions are logically necessary, since they follow from the premises, we should not regard them as stating what is physically necessary in actual life. The laws of supply and demand hold good for all markets, and generally speaking for districts where money economy has come into vogue; but they have not such absolute certainty as to enable us to predict the future course of affairs with any certainty, or to explain any phenomena of natural economy which survive.

There have been numerous histories of one or another department of economic activity, as for example merchant shipping, or agriculture, or of particular localities; but comparatively little progress has been made in surveying the growth of economic activities in their interconnection, and the development of the Body Economic as a whole. Indeed this involves many difficulties. The mass of influences at work appears to lose all coherence if it is separated from the framework which is given by the political history of one political community or another. There is, however, one purely economic conception which enables us to fix our attention on one thread in the complex economic development. Capital has been

spoken of as an historical category: it is the characteristic feature of modern times that capital has
attained complete dominance. If we fix our attention
on the conditions of industry when capital was unknown, on the circumstances which rendered the
formation of capital possible, and on its effectiveness
as a factor which undermined primitive organisations
and institutions, we shall find it possible to trace the
main changes in economic life and to call attention to
the more important survivals, without laying stress
on crises which are important for political purposes.
The economic history of a country cannot be the story
of steady and continuous progress all along the line,
for we are forced to realise at what great distances
of time the corresponding changes occurred in
different callings. The craftsman in a mediaeval
town was a small capitalist who worked for a market,
while subsistence farming has survived here and there
till modern times. The first examples of capitalists
who employed many workmen who would remain
wage-earners all their lives, are to be found in connection with the cloth trade; the struggle between
the large master who can procure the best equipment
and organisation, and the small master, is comparatively recent, and has come about with the
progress of mechanical inventions. In modern times
it becomes possible to trace the rise and decay of

different social institutions, which are consonant with
differences in the possession and employment of
capital.

All economic problems have two aspects, the
material resources which constitute the conveniences
and comforts of life on the one side, and the aims and
purposes which determine human beings in the use
they make of these resources on the other. There
is a material side, and there is a mental and moral
side; we have the best hope of distinguishing their
reaction upon one another if we endeavour to keep
them apart and not to blend them. The history of the
development of material resources, of the settlement
of land or the opening up of routes of commerce can
often be approximately dated; and we can also trace
the introduction of new aims and ideals and ambitions;
we can distinguish the cases where these aims could
be rendered effective by the action of a single human
being from those in which they depended for their
effectiveness on the working of institutions and
associations. By following out these distinctions we
may hope to get a scheme of Economic History that
is clear and definite, even though it does not borrow
the framework from political history.

(6) The word capital is commonly current in
a restricted sense when the questions of labour and

capital are under discussion; but it is important to notice that, for our present purpose, we must use the word in a wider sense as including commercial capital, and as meaning the fund of wealth which is employed with a view to obtaining an income. Capital may be sunk in land, as it was by men who acquired a hoard in the Middle Ages and used it to buy a rent charge[1], or in more modern times since the knowledge of agriculture has increased, in sinking money in permanent improvements by which the land may be rendered more productive. It is of course convenient for many purposes to treat the land, and questions connected with the land, apart from capital, but it is important that we should remember that cultivated land is what it is because capital has been sunk in it. There is also commercial capital, from which an income is derived by what were known in the Middle Ages as successful 'ventures'; and the aim of the merchant is to turn over his capital as rapidly as possible. Industrial capital, and all the developments of machinery and organisation which it has rendered possible, may for convenience be classed as a department of commercial capital and as belonging to monied men. There is also the capital of those who do not use their wealth themselves, but lend it to other people in return for the

[1] Ashley, *Introduction to Economic History*, I. pt. ii. 405.

promise to pay a regular income. All these are forms of capital, and different social groupings have arisen which would not have been possible unless capital had come into play in these various ways.

There are of course forms of social organisation which are appropriate to conditions in which capital does not exist at all; the formation of capital implies the existence of money economy. In countries and in circumstances where natural economy prevails, capital is unknown; but this helps us to notice what is on the whole the characteristic feature of capital; it is the factor which makes for progress. It is of supreme importance in all progressive societies; by the gradual introduction of capital in one or other department of economic life communities have, for good or for evil, been drawn out of contentment with a stationary state and led to enter on a path of material progress. In the study of early institutions it is of great interest to notice the precise points at which capital effected an entrance and undermined the social arrangements which were based on natural economy. In more advanced communities the amount of capital available and the methods in which it is used, are limiting conditions which control the development of social institutions.

The fact that capital has been the main instrument in material progress, enables us to distinguish its beneficial side clearly, from the incidental evils which have arisen in connection with its growth. Capital has enormously increased the power of man over nature; it has enabled him to wring far more from the soil, to introduce extraordinary aids in the manufacture of natural products for human use, and to provide the most wonderful facilities for intercommunication. By doing so it has greatly developed the wealth of communities and their opportunities of using that wealth for encouraging cultured human life; but at every stage of material progress there has been social hardship. The introduction of motors has been prejudicial to grooms and coachmen; and numberless illustrations could be given to show that in the march of progress individuals and classes have been sacrificed. This does not prove that progress is necessarily a bad thing, or that it should have been held back; but it does give us cause to consider the cost and sacrifice, through which every stage in progress has been attained. It is thus that every age has had its own social problem, in the effort to reconcile the progress of the community with the fair treatment of individuals.

(7) The story of the growth of capital is the material side of Economic History. It investigates what, at any place or time, were the materials and the

resources which were available for organisation; but we are also called upon to examine the objects and aims with which they were organised, and to enquire as to the ends and purposes which different human beings cherished at different times. Classical econo-mists were content to merge all other human aims in the desire for wealth; and though this may serve for the most advanced countries in recent times, it is necessary to discriminate, if we would understand the economic life of by far the greater part of mankind in the present day or would follow out the development of any one country.

It is of course true that strictly economic objects had been in view in connection with a great deal of organisation. The desire to make the most of material resources, and to obtain the greatest result for labour expended has underlain much of the social organisation of all ages; it has been the dominant aim in institutions for the formation and investment of capital which are such a prominent feature in modern society. Besides organisations for economic purposes institutions have been provided again and again which were intended to give fair play and equality of opportunity within each community. Such were many of the guilds and trading companies of the Middle Ages, or the national arrangements for the assessment of wages, according to the plenty or scarcity of the time, which were organised by Elizabeth. The social problems of each day have been different, the means of grappling with them have been different, and we cannot understand the story of the past unless we attempt to realise the precise problems of each age and the success or failure which attended human efforts to grapple with them.

This preliminary survey is a help to marking out the main divisions of our subject. There will be first of all the pre-capitalist organisation of society where natural economy is dominant. This stage may be spoken of as appropriate to the household; there is a second stage of organisation in cities, a social condition where natural economy has on the whole been superseded, and the use of money and the habit of marketing is familiar within the community; but capital has not been formed so generally as to affect the personal relations of the inhabitants to each other. Lastly we have a phase when the possession of capital and the habit of pushing trade has become dominant in all the institutions of society so that we have not only capital, but capitalism,—a social organisation which implies throughout the possession of capital. The convenience of these divisions, which have been drawn on economic grounds, is at least confirmed when we remember that they are also appropriate to an important geographical distinction as to the extent of the area which can be controlled. Household organisation applies for the most part to limited areas, or to an aggregate of limited areas. Civic organisation is applicable to a wider extension of territory, and to a highly complex economic life. National organisation can directly control the economic life of all the districts and towns within the realm, while it may indirectly, by international agreement, influence the economic conditions of the world as a whole. In making these divisions however, it must of course be remembered that they are not hard and fast compartments, into which the economic life of a country can be fitted, still less that the one immediately disappeared to make room for another to take its place. They must be thought of as types of organisation towards which actual institutions have tended to conform; but the transition from one stage to another has, for the most part, been gradual. It is not often that there has been such conscious struggle between the old and the new as to render the term revolution appropriate, still less are we justified in thinking that primitive institutions, when gradually superseded, must necessarily die out; on the other hand we have constantly to notice how long some institution or habit has lingered on after it had ceased to serve its original purpose. The complexity of modern society in Europe is due to the fact that there are so many survivals from the Middle Ages which have no analogues in new countries.

(8) The systematic study of Economic History may justify itself not only by widening the basis of observed facts, on which empirical economic science rests, but by the contribution it can offer both to History and to Social Philosophy. The historian may indeed be scandalised at the readiness of those, who are mainly interested in modern problems, to brush antiquarianism aside, and to concentrate interest on the genesis of modern conditions. When Prof. Cannan insists that Economic History should have some practical aim, and that " some moral, some lesson or guidance should be afforded by it[1]," the pragmatism of the economist will find little response among those who study history for its own sake. But the study of Economic History does after all react on the pursuit of historical investigation and especially on local history, and leads to the discriminating investigation of details which are of national importance. Not only so; if Economic History can give us a type of the development of the Body Economic, it places us in a position to compare the history of different countries, and to see how, from political

[1] *History of Local Rates in England*, p. 1.

or other causes, the forms which corresponding institutions take in different places have diverged from
the common type. Great Britain and Ireland have
been governed by one Crown and one Parliament,
but the Economic History of these nations has
been remarkably distinct. Though there is much
in the progress of England and Scotland that is
common to both countries alike, there are also
extraordinary differences. It is by comparing these
countries with one another that we can most easily
note the precise nature of the differences between
them; and we have need to be constantly on our
guard against assuming that the likeness is so close
that the course of development was practically the
same. The rural organisation and methods which
were dominant in England seem scarcely to have
penetrated to Scotland. The life of the towns and
the organisation of foreign commerce were curiously
distinct in mediaeval times; and since the Union,
Scotland has enjoyed remarkable economic independence and has been free to pursue her own
banking system and her own economic development
in accordance with her own ideas.

Economic History has also a contribution to make
to Social Philosophy. It is important for us to
recognise that freedom for the development of the
Body Economic is the most elementary of national

aspirations.   It was the great demand of the American colonies at the time when they declared their independence.   The bitterness of the present war has been due to the fact that so many peoples have felt that their economic freedom was threatened by the dominance of Germany, and they have formed the determination that they would not submit to be exploited in the interests of her industrial supremacy. Great Britain has learnt to forego the attempt to render the Colonies dependent on herself as parts of one Body Economic, she has granted to each of them freedom for organising their economic activity on the lines which were most promising for their own country, but even this principle has not been completely accepted; Ireland has always been thwarted and hampered in her aim for securing freedom to pursue her own economic prosperity.   In the seventeenth and eighteenth centuries the Whigs were jealous lest Ireland should become so wealthy as to yield a revenue to the Crown over which the British Parliament had no control[1]; when the Union of England and Ireland took place the *laissez faire* doctrine had so triumphed that any attempt to provide for the development of the Sister Kingdom seemed out of date[2].   The schemes for promoting the

---

[1] *English Historical Review*, I. 291.

[2] *Growth of English Industry and Commerce*, II. 592.

economic prosperity of Ireland which are associated with Sir Horace Plunkett's name, have been carelessly set aside, and the development of the economic prosperity of Ireland has been delayed.

The outbreak of the present war has awakened a large number of the people of Great Britain to the fact that there is a danger lest the economic independence of this country should be undermined by a rival nation. Many men in all classes are ready to recognise that it would be well to take the steps that may be needed to preserve the economic conditions of political independence. What we claim for ourselves we should be willing to concede to each of the other countries which form the British Empire. It is vain to think that the Irish will be satisfied with any measure of self-government, as long as the opportunity of developing the economic resources and activities of the country, in accordance with their own aspirations, is withheld.

II. THE DEVELOPMENT OF THE BODY ECONOMIC IN ENGLAND

PART I. PRE-CAPITALIST ORGANISATION

(i) *Natural Economy*

(9) The most primitive organisation with which we become acquainted in England is the household; there was no buying or selling within the community, but the duties of each member were assigned, and the available food was shared by those who had part in the life of the community. The material possessions of these households were lands, either unoccupied lands which the members of the community could cultivate, or waste lands which they could use for pasturage. The aim and purpose with which this wealth was used differed in different cases. The royal household, and those of other potentates, were organised with a view to effectiveness as a military force; but far more interesting, from the economic standpoint, are the great monastic communities. They were founded with a view to maintaining the service of God and the honour of one of His saints;

and the resources of the community were devoted to
these religious objects. For hundreds of years a great
part of the economic vigour of England was directed
to purposes which many would now denounce as
superstitious: but there was a marvellous development
of economic activity which resulted in the erection of
magnificent churches and monastic buildings throughout the length and breadth of the land. These
monasteries were organised with the hope of presenting religion as dignified and prosperous, and internally
the community spirit was strong; but they were
established in surroundings where money economy
and capital gradually came into play more and more.
Their power of adapting themselves to these changed
conditions was limited, and eventually the communities failed to hold their own and were broken up. We
may see the steps in this process more clearly when
we come to discuss the changes which have taken
place in the management of landed property.

(10) Our knowledge of the early periods of
monastic life in Europe is mostly derived from the
Benedictine Rule and from legends. It is not easy
to apply modern economic distinctions with any
precision, but we shall not be far wrong if we think
of the early monasteries as communities in which
each inmate was assigned his special task and where all

shared alike in common meals. There was no attempt
to distinguish one brother from another according to
the result of his work; there was a common table and
they fared alike. According to the Benedictine Rule
two dishes with salad or dessert in season were to form
the principal meal and each monk was to be given a
loaf of bread for the day; while meat and wine were
to be allowed at the discretion of the Abbot for those
who required them, either because of the arduousness
of their labours or on account of physical infirmities[1].
No distinction was made according to the value of
the service rendered, but modifications were permitted
according to the need of the recipient; from this point
of view the man who undertook most drudgery had
a claim to indulgence, rather than the man whose
employment involved most taste and skill. The good
management of the monastery, on its material side,
consisted in getting each labourer to do his allotted
task thoroughly and well; and the atmosphere of
exacting labour was far more analogous to that of a
Roman villa with its slave labour and ergastula, than
to a modern business, where each man is free to try to
get what he is worth and where increased pay is
offered to stimulate to more diligent labour.

Though the monasteries engaged in great undertakings, such as the clearing of their lands and the

[1] *Regula*, Migne, lxvi. col. 613, 641.

building of churches, they had not any capital, as we
understand the term; they might agree to assign
some of their income regularly to permanent improvements, and this would serve the purpose of capital;
but they had not a "fund of wealth" which was
available for continued operations. In any bad year,
not to mention times of famine, they would have
no surplus income, and building operations would
necessarily cease.

(11) From the ninth century onwards, however,
we come across traces which seem to show that certain
monastic communities, in their corporate capacity,
were in possession of capital; they were engaged in
distant commerce and owned ships. The articles
which they imported were not entirely for sale, but
were used instead to replenish their own stores; still
the monasteries were regularly engaged in the shipping
business. There is evidence that in 779 Charlemagne
freed the factors and the ships of the Abbeys of St
Germain-en-Laye from toll in Rouen, Amiens, Utrecht,
and other towns, while the privilege of having a free
ship was accorded to the Abbey of St Mesmin near
Orleans by Clovis[1]. English monasteries do not seem
to have been so actively engaged in shipping, but we

---

[1] Ernest de Freville, *Mémoire sur le Commerce maritime
de Rouen*, I. 55.

hear more about trade in Scotland. The monks of Scone received a letter of protection for a ship belonging to them from Alexander II[1], and a considerable trade seems to have been done by the monks of the Isle of May[2]. Abundant evidence shows that, in the thirteenth century, English monks, especially the Cistercians, did an enormous business in the sale of wool[3]; they do not, however, seem to have engaged in shipping themselves, but to have sold fleeces to Flemish or Italian merchants.

There are also signs of the introduction of industrial capital. In the eleventh century the old tradition seems to have been retained. The great monastery at Hirschau, Würtemberg, was regarded as a model establishment where industry of every sort was carried on, apparently on a basis of natural economy, by the monks themselves and the associated lay brothers[4]. But though the monks maintained a great building tradition[5] it does not seem that many of them continued to work as craftsmen. The monastery began to employ hired labour. The stone which was required in 1067 for the building

[1] *Liber Ecclesiae de Scon* (Bannatyne Club), p. 45.

[2] Chalmers, *Caledonia* (1782), II. 51.

[3] *Growth of English Industry*, I. 629.

[4] C. D. Christman, *Geschichte des Klosters Hirschau*, 58.

[5] William of Sens was chosen at Canterbury in 1174, after a great consultation of artificers (Gervase of Canterbury, R. S. I. 6).

of St Augustine's at Canterbury was imported ready worked from Caen[1]. When we come to the fifteenth century there is documentary evidence that money payments had come into vogue at Canterbury; while we find that new works of any importance were undertaken by contractors who found the staff of men, or 'artificers of the Lodge,' that were temporarily employed. These masons, who moved from place to place according as stone buildings were being executed, were organised as a migratory national craft, and differed in many of their rights and privileges from the municipal craft guilds[2].

(12) In contrast to the monastic households we have the royal and baronial households, which were not organised for purposes of production so much as with a view to consumption. The King and his court had their duties in the government of the realm and its defence, and were settled in castles; though the royal household itself, which was organised with a reference to the maintenance of the King and his officers, was constantly migratory, as were those of

[1] *Acta S. S.*, May 26, 401 f.

[2] The Goldsmiths' craft had been so closely connected with the issue of coins that it had also something of this migratory character. For fuller details see my notes on the "Organisation of the Masons' Craft in England" in *Proceedings of the British Academy*, VI.

the nobles who did not maintain one settled residence like a monastery.   When there were few roads it was easier to take the family to the food and to eat up the stores that had been accumulated in different places than to collect all the food for one centre.   Men with great estates in different parts of the country, bishops, barons, as well as the King himself, worked out the calendar for the year and stayed at the castle on one of their estates for as long a time as the produce of that estate would allow.   Robert Grosseteste has drawn up some interesting rules for household management which are based upon this as the best method of management[1]. The economic necessity for constant migration explains one reason why the King with his household was so frequently upon the move as the dates of charters show.   It also helps to explain why episcopal palaces were so numerous.   The Bishop of Ely had one palace at Wisbech, another at Downham, another at Ely, and another at Balsham, and the bishop moved from one palace to another as his household ate up the products of one estate and then went on to the next.

These migratory households, especially the royal household, must have done something to diffuse a money economy in their various environments.   In the East the caravans are a sort of migratory market,

---

[1] *Walter of Henley*, edited by E. Lamont, p. 122.

which sell goods and buy supplies at any point where they halt. In a similar fashion the royal households were constantly needing to supplement supplies which they procured from the royal estates. Among the officials in the tenth and eleventh centuries were moneyers, who furnished the coins with which purchases could be made, and all through the Middle Ages we hear of purveyors and their exactions. They went about demanding goods, and if they paid for them at all they rarely paid full market prices. It was only after the Restoration that the practice was brought to an end and it was not formally abolished till 1780.

It is thus that these two types of household have left behind them the beginnings of two different forms of economic organisation. In the monastery, stress was laid on the organisation of work; the hours of work, and the conditions of maintenance assigned to labour. In the royal household on the other hand, attention was directed to the prevention of waste and the conditions of purchase; the Assize of Bread and Ale, and the regulation of Weights and Measures would be of great importance to a migratory household which was accustomed to rely on the purchase of supplies.

(ii) *Subsistence farming and the introduction of*
       Capital in the Management of Land

(13) Agricultural occupations lend themselves
most naturally to natural economy; household
organisation was deeply rooted in the management of
land, so as to hold its own as an active, and latterly
as an obstructive agent. The change from the
natural economy which existed at the time of the
Conquest, to the capitalist system which had come
into complete possession at the beginning of the nineteenth century, is spread over a period of eight
centuries. The agriculturist in the early Norman
times was occupied in securing a subsistence, and
agriculture was organised with a view to subsistence
farming. The land management of the nineteenth
century aimed at working for an outside market, and
was, therefore, engaged in improvements which
rendered the land productive of the crops for which
there was a sale. It was compatible with a constant
effort at improvement, while subsistence farming had
given no similar stimulus to economic progress.

There was also a great social or constitutional
difference between the agricultural organisation at the
earlier and at the later time. The agricultural community of the early Middle Ages was controlled by the
lord of the manor and his officials, though the villeins

had also a voice in regard to certain matters. As time went on the direct interference[1] of the lord and his officials in the management of land diminished, and the part played by the community seems to have become relatively more important, at all events in retarding economic changes. In the nineteenth century the business was conducted on capitalist lines; part of the capital was sunk in land or buildings by the landlord, whilst part belonged to the tenant farmer who worked the land; and the disabilities from which the labourers suffered at the time of the Swing Riots and later[2], were troubles that could only have arisen under a regime of capitalism.

In the revolution, which occurred through the transition from the household organisation of the twelfth century to the capitalist system of the nineteenth, we may distinguish several stages, and even illustrate them and date them approximately. Further investigation will doubtless render it possible to characterise each stage more fully, and to date the dominance of each more precisely for different parts of the country; but this will serve, at all events, as a useful working hypothesis.

---

[1] "On the office of Steward." J. Smyth, *Lives of the Berkeleys*, I. Preface, p. ii.

[2] *Growth*, II. 687. For the last revolt in 1830 see Hammond, *Village Labourer*, p. 240.

(14) The eleventh century manor, as it is described in the *Domesday Book* and as its organisation is detailed by later authorities, such as the *Hundred Rolls* and numberless bailiffs' accounts, was not only a unit for fiscal purposes and the collection of taxation, but a unit for the organisation of agriculture. The agriculture had two sides, one or other of which might be more developed in different parts of the country; but attention to both was necessary, and they played into each other's hands. The maintenance of stock on the waste was necessary, not only to plough the land, but also as the chief means of procuring manure; while the aftermath on the stubble assisted in the maintenance of the stock during the autumn and winter months. The lord and the villagers formed one community and co-operated together; the centre of all the operations was the domain farm, which was managed for the lord by his bailiff. This consisted of strips in the open field, the produce of which was devoted to the lord's use; and the work on these fields was done by the villeins with their teams, who were remunerated by the possession of other arable strips which they could work in their own time. There seem at first[1] to have been no money payments between the villeins and the lord, although as time

[1] *Growth*, I. 76, 79. "Rectitudines Singularum Personarum," in Thorpe, *Ancient Laws*, I. 432.

went on a larger and larger proportion of the actual services appear to be discharged in money.

Besides these services, the tenantry were required to make certain small payments in kind, as eggs or poultry; and those at least who owned any part of a plough-team, had pasture rights for their stock on the waste and in the assignment of meadow, which were respected. The lord of the manor had very large powers over the land in which the village was situated; this power was not arbitrary, however, as the custom of the village could not be easily set aside; and the same rotation of crops, which usually consisted of wheat, barley and fallow, was practically maintained, both on the domain farm and on the tenants' holdings as well. The whole of the open fields were worked on the same system, while all the stock, belonging either to the lord or his tenants, was free to run upon the common waste. Such was the primitive condition of affairs, which seems to have held good in its main features throughout the greater part of England. During its dominance there was little opportunity for change or improvement. The population increased but slowly, and there was little means of giving employment to increased labour and little incentive to obtain larger crops. Agriculture was on the whole stationary; and it appears that the system of fallowing, which was probably inherited from the time of the

Roman occupation, together with the manure procur-
able from the stock, rendered it possible to continue
this system from decade to decade with comparatively
little exhaustion of the soil[1]. In regard to such matters,
however, there must have been great differences in
different parts of the country. It seems that in
Scotland fallowing was but little practised until the
seventeenth or eighteenth century[2]; and it also appears
that the domain farm occupied a much less important
place in Scottish husbandry than in England generally.
It may be doubted whether there was any class of
villeins on Scottish estates who were responsible
for the regular week work on domain farms; the
local institutions were not so highly developed as to
be an obstacle to a general change after the Union,
and there do not seem to have been any communal
rights to hamper the efforts of Napier of Merchiston[3]
and of other seventeenth century improvers north of
the Tweed.

(15) The thirteenth and early fourteenth centuries were a period of extraordinary economic progress in England; the Crusades had given a stimulus
to commerce, and a number of towns had extended

---

[1] T. Stone, *Huntingdonshire*, p. 9.
[2] *Scottish Historical Review* (January, 1916), L. 180.
[3] M. Napier, *Memories of John Napier*, p. 284.

their borders, while others had been founded. The development of commerce and industry seems to have reacted upon agriculture, and to have opened up markets for agricultural produce. Tillage and pasture farming were carried on less exclusively for subsistence than before; there were opportunities for sale, which rendered the lords of the manors anxious to manage their lands on the best methods and thus obtain better produce and a larger income[1]. A very full account of the habits of the improvers of the time is given in the *Lives of the Berkeleys*. Thomas the second, lord of Berkeley (1281–1321) used to go in progress from one of his manor and farm houses to another scarce two miles asunder, making stay at each of them and then back to his standing house, where his wife and family remained[2]. His wife, Joan, spent much of her time in supervising her dairy affairs, passing from farm house to farm house and sometimes taking account of the smallest details[3]. The tradition of minute care was maintained by their successors. Thomas the third, lord of Berkeley (1326–1361), farmed on a gigantic scale[4]. Few or no great fairs or

[1] Hubert Hall, *Pipe Roll of Bishopric of Winchester*, 1207–8, p. xxv and App.

[2] J. Smyth, *Lives of the Berkeleys*, I. 164.

[3] J. Smyth, *op. cit.* I. 206.

[4] Mr R. E. Prothero (*English Farming*, p. 45) summarises his operations thus. He kept in his own hands the domains of

markets were in these parts whereat this lord was not himself, as at Wells, Gloucester, Winchcomb, Tetbury and others; where also he now bought or changed the several grains that sowed his arable lands[1]. Incidental evidence from other districts shows that there were great landlords who could organise the carrying of their produce to distant markets. The abbot of Ramsey appears to have supplied the London markets by road[2], and also to have sent corn for shipment at Lynn. During this period, though there was no great change in the knowledge of the arts, the profit from

upwards of 75 manors stocking them with his own oxen, cows, sheep and swine; on no manor did the flock of sheep number less than 300, on some it reached 1500. At Beverston in Gloucestershire in the seventh year of Edward III, he sheared 5775 sheep. From these manors his supplies were drawn to feed each day at his "standing house" 300 persons and 100 horses. Thence came every year geese, ducks, peacocks, capons, hens and chickens—200 of each kind, many thousands of eggs and a thousand pigeons coming from a single manor—stores of honey, wax and nuts and "uncredible" number of oxen, bullocks, calves, sheep and lambs, and vast quantities of wheat, rye, barley, oats, pease, beans, apples and pears. All was accounted for with minute care by the stewards, reeves, and bailiffs. Their accounts for the manors and for the household show what amount of corn remained in the granary from the previous year; how much was each year reaped and winnowed, sold at markets, shipped to sea; how much was consumed in the lord's house, in his stable, in his kennels, in the poultry yard, or in the falcons' mews; how much was malted; how much was given to the poor, to friars and other religious orders by way of yearly allowance.

[1] J. Smyth, *Lives of the Berkeleys*, I. 300.
[2] *Cart. Monast. de Ramseia*, R.S. II. 17; III. 302.

farming seems to have increased greatly on the estates
of the Bishop of Winchester[1]. This improvement
was apparently due to the increased area taken into
cultivation, and possibly to enclosures in severalty[2]
and to the care and attention which were given to
bailiff farming, in the effort to cater, not merely for
the lord's subsistence, but for outside markets. The
various books which were compiled on the subject of
husbandry, as well as the masses of ministers accounts
which survive, help to show how widely this increased
interest was diffused.

(16) The period of prosperity appears to have
come to an end with the Black Death. There were
great difficulties in obtaining labour and in maintaining
the system of bailiff farming; owing to the diminished
population there must have been a decreased demand
for corn so that it would be less remunerative to send
it to market; and farming came once more to be
mainly practised with a view to subsistence. The
lords of the manor were no longer ready to take a
personal interest in the management of the land, but
were glad to commute all obligations from their
tenants for money payments, and to sell their own
privileges, for pasturage and the like, on the best terms

[1] Hall, *op. cit.* p. xx.
[2] Smyth, *Lives of the Berkeleys*, I. 113.

they could get. Bailiff farming fell into disuse, and this seems to have had a serious effect on the standard of agriculture throughout the country. The lords found their interest, not in maintaining a high condition of tillage but in securing money rentals from their estates. From the Peasants' Revolt "began the times to alter and he with them (much occasioned by the insurrection of Wat Tyler and generally of all the Commons in the land). And then instead of manuring his domains in each manor with his own servants, oxen, kine, sheep, swine, poultry and the like, under the oversight of the Reeves of the manors ...this lord began to joyst and take in other mens cattle into his pasture grounds by the week, month, and quarter: and to sell his meadow grounds by the acre....And after, in the time of Henry IV, let out by the year still more and more by the acre as he found chapmen and price to his liking[1]."

It is probable that during the fifteenth and sixteenth centuries there was a deterioration of arable fields owing to the exhaustion of the soil, and it is certain that there was neglect on the part of the lords and their agents in regard to the common pastures. In some few cases this may have been counteracted by activity on the part of tenants in the management of the waste, but the very occasional evidence

[1] Smyth, *Lives of the Berkeleys*, II. 5–6.

which survives does not lead us to suppose that this was very frequently the case; though we read of a summons to a town meeting in 1368[1], and of a committee of six[2] being selected for ordering the affairs of the community[3]. But it does not appear that these complicated matters were properly taken in hand generally, though in the time of Elizabeth and James I there were villages in Cambridgeshire which were at considerable expense in obtaining legal powers for the management of the common waste and the stock upon it[4]. In the seventeenth century generally it appears that through want of regulation and organisation, the facilities for pasturage on the common waste were not as valuable as they had formerly been.

(17) The remedy, which was probably adopted by enterprising individuals in self defence, was recommended for general introduction by Fitzherbert,

[1] *Halimota Prioratus Dunelmensis*, Surtees Society, LXXXII. 70.

[2] *Ibid.* p. 82.

[3] This would include questions as to the amount of pasturage available for the tenantry (*ibid.* p. 12), questions as to the right to put stock on the common (p. 17), questions of meadow closes and separate pastures and questions of the treatment of horses and oxen. There was a common course of cultivation at Willington (p. 105), and a common fold at Aycliffe (p. 104).

[4] "Common Rights at Cottenham and Stretham in Cambridgeshire," in *Camden Miscellany*, XII. 178.

who published his book on Surveying in 1523[1]. He recommends the withdrawal of the husband who would thrive from the common fields and common pasturage altogether, and shows that he would be in every way better off if he had separate closes which he could use as he liked for maintaining his stock and for growing crops. By convertible husbandry he could keep his cattle separate from infection by other stock, and could look after them properly; while he could also save the manure and use it for his own fields. In this way the small capitalist, who had withdrawn from the custom of the village because his own land was enclosed, was able to make his keeping of stock and his growing of corn work together for a better result. Those who were able to adopt this system were also able to take advantage of the facilities for the sale of agricultural produce which became increasingly frequent in the sixteenth century.

(18) The Elizabethan period was a time of revival of trade and industry in many ways, and this once again, as in the thirteenth century, reacted on agriculture. There were facilities for export of which Burghley was anxious that the realm should take advantage[2]; but even more striking is the increase of

---

[1] *Growth*, I. 553.
[2] *Ibid.* II. 87.

internal communication and the regulation of a corn trade within the realm. Towns in their earlier days had obtained their main supplies from their own fields[1], but this was no longer possible for London at any rate; and the demand of London ramified for a considerable distance. Farnham[2] became a local centre where corn was sold, which ultimately found its way to the London market; and the building of corn exchanges and new market halls in such towns as Shrewsbury shows that the business was at least being conducted on a larger scale. The regulations, which were made by the Council for the clerks of the market[3] for corn bodgers, and other persons engaged in the trade, show how widely it was diffused; and it is probably true to say that in England generally agriculture passed, in Elizabeth's time, from being an occupation which was mainly pursued for the sake of subsistence and became a trade which was carried on by capitalists who looked for their profit to prices in the market.

Dymock, an agricultural expert of the seventeenth century, looked back to the time of Elizabeth as the beginning of improved husbandry[4]; and the capitalists, who farmed land in severalty apart from the common custom, were not only able to do better than

---

[1] F. W. Maitland, *Township and Borough*, p. 52.
[2] O. Manning, *Surrey*, III. 131.   [3] *Growth*, II. 94.
[4] *Ibid.* II. 100, but see p. 43 above.

their neighbours with their corn growing and their stock, but they were also able to introduce any new crops that seemed likely to answer well. Intercourse with the Low Countries led to the adoption of many improvements from Flanders. Experiments were made in root crops[1]; though clover and artificial grasses were strongly recommended, they did not come into general use till a much later period. The process of improvement which had been noticeable in the sixteenth and seventeenth centuries was carried on with great enthusiasm in the eighteenth, by Townsend and Jethro Tull. Bakewell[2] improved the breeds of cattle; and more attention was given to the rotation of crops and the cultivation of the special varieties which were suitable to each soil. King George III, the Duke of Bedford, and Mr Coke of Holkham, were all great enthusiasts in regard to practical farming and set an example which found many imitators among the members of the Royal Agricultural Society.

All these steps were taken by men who had capital to invest, and none of them were possible so long as the customary tillage and customary neglect of the common waste were allowed to go on. Arthur Young and the agricultural writers of the times felt strongly that common fields and common custom

[1] *Growth*, II. 546.   [2] *Ibid.* II. 551.

were a bar to improvement of any kind, and that no
real advance in agriculture could be expected until
there was a general enclosure. There can be no doubt
whatever that, through these successive changes, an
extraordinary economic gain has come about, and that
infinitely more is made of the landed resources of the
country than was the case at the time of the Norman
Conquest. This is true both as regards the production
of corn and the feeding of sheep or of cattle; through
the exertions of these generations of improvers there
has been an enormous increase of national wealth.
This plain fact is sometimes ignored or forgotten[1] by
those who look at the story from the other side, and
lay stress on the incidental loss which has accompanied
these changes. That incidental loss has been a real
thing; it is well that we should face it and see clearly
the price we have paid for these economic improvements; we shall then be in a position to estimate
whether we have paid too dearly for them or not.

(19) It is important to look at this transition not
only from the economic side, but from the social point
of view as well. Government recognised the advantages
that came economically, and measures were passed for
giving a better market for corn in Elizabeth's time, and

---

[1] Hammond, *Village Labourer*, p. 26.

also by the Corn Bounty Act of William and Mary[1];
but the government also realised that there were social
difficulties against which it was necessary to give
some protection.   There had been extensive social
legislation in the period of disintegration and neglect
which followed the Black Death; an attempt was
made to check those who were taking advantage of
a national calamity in order to obtain excessive payment for their services; and the machinery for the
assessment of wages, which lasted in one form or other
till 1814, had its beginning at this time.   There was
also a strong feeling against depopulators[2], and those
who gave over their land to the maintenance of large
flocks, so as neither to supply food stuffs, for the
flocks were chiefly kept for their wool, nor to give employment.   Numerous laws were enacted, and various
commissions collected evidence and endeavoured to
redress the grievance which arose in this connection.
The improvers, like Fitzherbert, were inclined to argue
that the change to convertible husbandry in severalty
was beneficial all round, and that the only persons
who lost by enclosing were the shiftless and idle; but
this was not true in the eighteenth century, and it is
not likely to have been true at an earlier period; the
impression remains that in many cases the enclosure
was carried through in a high-handed manner, without

[1] *Growth*, II. 541.   [2] *Ibid.* II. 102 n.

sufficient consideration of the expense in which the smaller farmers were involved, and without due regard for the position of the very poor.

There were, however, not a few measures which were intended to give relief to the sufferers by the change. The Elizabethan movement for preventing the building of cottages, unless four acres of ground should be assigned[1] them, and indeed all the machinery for the employment of the poor, were called into being by the social mischiefs that accompanied the process of enclosure. That these measures of redress did not deal adequately with the social problems which had arisen is true enough, but it is clear that Parliament made an effort to minimise the social mischiefs which were occasioned by the material progress of the nation. In retrospect it may be doubted whether it would have been wiser to stop material progress in order to enable those who were habituated to an improvident tradition to continue in their old ways[2].

Enquiries as to the social effects of enclosure are complicated by the mischief which was due to other causes, such as the industrial changes of the early

[1] 31 El. c. 7.

[2] Rural progress in the eighteenth century appeared to have been extraordinarily different in Scotland and England. In Scotland, where we hear little or nothing of a common custom, there was far less difficulty in pressing forward improvements.

nineteenth century and the dying out of village industries. In the sixteenth, seventeenth, and eighteenth
centuries, there seems to have been a considerable
diffusion of manufacturing industry in rural districts.
The spinning of wool and the weaving of cloth were
practised in many counties, so that the village householder had two strings to his bow; the result of the
invention of the power loom and the spinning-jenny
was the withdrawal of the opportunity of industrial
employment from the rural population; they had to
depend entirely upon what they could earn from the
land and they could no longer eke out their income by
manufacturing. The invention of machinery denuded
the rural districts of what had been profitable occupations, and subsequent changes have told against the
village tradesman, and have put industry and retail
dealing more entirely into the hands of townsmen.
These changes have made a considerable difference to
rural life; though they synchronised with the rapid
progress of enclosure after the passing of the General
Act, they are not to be regarded as evils which were
incidental to this particular change, and must not be
included in summing up the cost paid for material
progress in agriculture. On the whole the rural
history illustrates the enormous power of capital in
bringing about the increase of material wealth, while
it also gives illustrations of the social cost in the

decay of the yeomanry which was involved in this material progress.

The process of enclosure, and the transition from the old subsistence farming of the yeomen to farming for the market, went on for more than a century. The special motives for enclosure at any particular time, and the manner in which it was carried out, can only be thoroughly discussed as a matter of local history. Cambridgeshire offers an extraordinarily good field for these investigations as the process of enclosure was belated, and took place at the end of the eighteenth century and beginning of the nineteenth[1]. We have besides remarkably accurate information as to the nature of the agricultural changes and the effects on the population, and these were put on record by skilled observers. Detailed information in regard to this one district helps us to see more clearly what had been going on in other counties in regard to which we have scantier records.

(20) That there was a national economic gain is undoubted, and this national economic gain was also a personal gain to the land-owning classes of the community. The fact that the soil of the nation was put to better uses and rendered more and more productive, is often left out of sight; and the landlords are

[1] *Cambridgeshire Materials for the History of Agriculture* in *Proc. of Camb. Antiq. Soc.* No. LXVIII.

represented as if they were thinking merely of their personal gain and were careless about everything else. It certainly appears as if this was true in the sixteenth century, when so many parishes were depopulated and sheep farming gradually extended at the expense of tillage[1]. The production of wool was remunerative to a large number of the gentry, but it was not beneficial to the nation, as it neither provided opportunities for the maintenance of a large population on the land nor contributed to the national supply of food to any considerable extent. Parliamentary and royal authority combined to pass and enforce measures which should be unfavourable for the operations of depopulators; but the matter was entirely different when any enclosing was undertaken for the purposes of improved husbandry, and those who were bringing about a definite increase of national resources were not condemned for making personal gain through their introduction of a public improvement. Improving landlords in the seventeenth century had the duty of public spirited action constantly impressed on them in a way that is little known in the present day. In so far as the desire of increased rental was a principal motive in the eighteenth century, it was blended with a public spirited desire to do the best thing for the country.

[1] *Growth*, II. 88, 102.

There seems to be little doubt that the yeoman farmers and peasantry suffered by the change and were reduced to poverty. In some cases they appear to have been the victims of legal chicanery, both in the sixteenth[1] and the eighteenth centuries[2], and to have been ousted from their hereditary possessions by wealthy land grabbers. Where wrongs of this sort were done, there is no excuse; and the economic gain cannot be rightly regarded as palliating the injustice. It seems likely that these cases were frequent enough to give rise to the bitterness between class and class which we find in the early nineteenth century. But there are cases which are more doubtful, where the impoverishment and decay of the small tenants was the direct result of the removal of the obstacle to better farming. The combining of strips in the open fields into several holdings was a difficult task, as both the quality and quantity of land had to be taken into account, and the valuation of the pasture rights on the waste attached to each holding was also a com-plicated business. The whole process was exceedingly difficult and the smaller tenants had not the means of paying their quota of the expense or of making the necessary outlay for fencing. The change may have

---

[1] Ashley, *Introduction to English Economic History*, I. ii. 275.

[2] *Growth*, II. 558.

been remunerative to wealthy men in places where many of the tenants could not afford the preliminary expenses of the change.

That the labourers suffered is generally recognised; their rights on the common waste were for the most part insignificant when calculated in terms of money, though the cows' grass had been of inestimable value in the maintaining of the family. It was also true that for many of the advantages which labourers possessed, they could show no proper title; their privileges had been carelessly allowed to grow up during the century when the regulation of commons had fallen into disuse. But the fact that these privileges might depend on customs of no long standing did not diminish the sense of grievance in being deprived of them. Another difficulty, which told against the poorer classes, was the fact that land when improved could be put to better uses, and that this necessitated changes of occupation on the part of the rural population. This was most obviously true in the Cambridgeshire fens and in Lincolnshire, where the inhabitants had been to a large extent their own masters[1] and spent their time in fishing and fowling and horse breeding. The change by which they were forced to adapt themselves to the routine of agriculture was not a popular one; it may be doubted in some

[1] *Growth*, II. 115.

cases whether those who pushed on this movement were well advised economically. The enormous cost at which the change was carried through and the loss of the old products of the fens must be taken into account when the gain either nationally or personally is reckoned up. In such cases it may be possible to weigh the economic gain, and to ask the question whether it was really worth while to force on those stalwart races a change of occupation. In many parts of the country in the eighteenth century, changes of occupation of a less striking character were very frequent. The progress of enclosure was forced on from a desire to increase the corn supply of the country and corn growing. The small farmers were for the most part occupied, so far as the markets were concerned, in dairy farming and stock raising[1], though they might do a little subsistence farming for themselves. The tendency was for corn growing to be developed, and those who had maintained themselves as small farmers in the old days had neither the capital nor the skill to adapt themselves to the new conditions except by being merged in the ranks of the labourers. This was the most serious of all the social changes ; it seems to have taken place in connection with enclosing[2] as the line between the capitalist farmer and

---

[1] H. Levy, *Large and Small Holdings*.

[2] Prof. Gonner (*Common land and Enclosure*, p. 396) shows

the labourer who worked for wages was drawn more definitely than before, and the rural labourer was not only deprived of independence as his own master, but also of the opportunities which he had had for rising in the world.

Just because the introduction of capitalism in land management was so gradual and so long continued, it is specially instructive. The introduction of new machinery and the organisation and the re-organisation of textile or other industries proceed very rapidly and almost by a series of crises. The gain to the nation and to the capitalist, by the introduction of machinery, is more obvious than it was in the case of enclosing, while the loss can be represented as merely transitory and something that is soon defrayed by the expansion of business. But the gain from the intervention of capital in the management of land was less obvious and the loss of status to certain classes of the community has been permanent. It is not wise to try to stop the march of progress, but it is important that we should see as clearly as possible what the march of progress costs.

(21) It would be a mistake, however, to suppose that even though there has been such long continued

that the material loss of the labourers has been exaggerated, but the loss of opportunities is an evil that cannot be estimated.

progress on the part of capitalism, subsistence farming is even now wholly extinct; there are elements of subsistence farming which survive among the holders of allotments and small holdings who do not seek a market for their produce, but who use their land to provide vegetables for the household or food for poultry. Even in large farms the household is often provided with dairy produce, and there are many parts of the country where those who do not keep a cow are unable to procure milk for their own consumption. The conditions of farming also involve much less fluidity of labour than the industrial wage earner expects; the farmer must rely on having men on the spot to look after the stock, and accommodation in cottages is in consequence assigned to responsible labourers. The relation between the master and the man cannot be satisfactorily expressed as a mere cash nexus.

While these elements of subsistence farming and the household organisation of work still survive, there has been, during the last half century, a great check to the conditions which attracted capital to land and stimulated agricultural progress. In the seventeenth century much attention was paid to the facilities for marketing corn, but there has been no similar care for tillage in the present day. Owing to the changes of communication, which became noticeable in the last

decades of the nineteenth century, the home market
has been greatly affected by American competition;
and the corn grower is not able to count on getting a
remunerative price.   Facilities for communication and
railway rates have also acted prejudicially in regard
to potatoes, green vegetables and fruit, while at the
same time the burden of taxation has greatly increased;
this has been largely due to the increased obligations
in regard to education, roads, and provision for the
aged and the poor.   But this means that there is great
difficulty in making land a profitable investment.
The old system of subsistence farming has almost
entirely disappeared; but in so far as a new system
of small holdings has been introduced, it has not been
able to command the conditions which would make
for the good management of the soil.

Part II.   The Progress of Capitalism in Mediaeval Cities

(i)   *Their Economic Prosperity*

(22)   The life of mediaeval cities has been invested
with many elements of romance; the civic culture of
the Italians is among the most important features of
the Middle Ages, and when we look at the relics which
survive, we feel that the towns were an important
feature in Mediaeval England.   London has suffered

from the devastation of the Great Fire, so that there
is little which remains to help us to picture its magnifi-
cence in the fourteenth century; but the town of York
still gives us a conception of a great centre of wealth
and power. It has a Castle and a Cathedral and
Abbey, and it was also protected by magnificent walls;
its Guildhall suggests that its mayors lived in great
state; and the Hall of the Merchant Adventurers
indicates the importance of its trade. Norwich and
Ipswich, Exeter and Coventry, have vestiges which
tell of their long continued importance and prosperity.

The city as a social organism had two main features,
which distinguish it from the household. Natural
economy had been practically superseded, and money
economy had become habitual within the group itself,
not only, as in the case of monasteries, in its relation
with the outside world; but besides this the inhabitants enjoyed self-government. The aim which they
set before themselves was the continued prosperity of
the town itself, and the householder had a status as
a member of this self-governing community.

These characteristic features distinguish the fully
developed city from pre-capitalist types, but they are
not so precise that we are able to classify all the towns,
in their various stages of development, with perfect
certainty; it is enough to say that the towns approxi-
mated to a type of organisation that was appropriate

to capitalism. So far as economic life is concerned, the household of each free townsman still retained many of the features of natural economy, though it was no longer independent since it was absorbed in the larger life of the town. The servants and apprentices boarded with the master, and received the main reward of their work in kind, though the master bought his materials and sold his goods for money. It is still harder to draw a hard and fast line in regard to self-government. The constitutional history of different towns shows how long the struggle for self-government continued and how step by step the towns obtained charters[1] which gave them additional freedom from the control of manor or royal officers. Such a town as Manchester obviously enjoyed a great deal of practical self-government under a manorial constitution[2]. The turning point probably consisted in the obtaining of such economic independence as enabled them to pursue a policy of their own, so as to manage their affairs with reference to the prosperity of the town itself, and not in subordination to the needs of any other social group, like the castle and its lord, or the monastery under the shadow of which the town had originally grown. Lay lords appear on the whole to have been willing to sell their powers for

---

[1] *Growth*, I. 211.
[2] *Ibid*. I. 214.

definite rentals, but a resident body such as a monastery does not seem to have been so ready to refrain from interfering with the community that had grown up at its doors. The era of the Crusades was the great period when towns obtained charters from kings and nobles, but the bitter struggles between the townsmen and the monks at Norwich and Bury and Reading lasted long after this time[1]. One of the grievances which led to the Peasants' Revolt was that the monks of St Albans[2] were refusing to allow the townsmen to use hand mills, and thus were interfering with the economic independence of the inhabitants of the town, and treating them as tenants who were thirled to the lord's mill.

(23) The early town, as we come across it in the twelfth and thirteenth centuries, had important material resources. Many had large fields from which important supplies could be drawn and they were for the most part agricultural communities[3]. The early history of many towns seems to turn on the privileges of the landed men and the attempts of other inhabitants to shake off their dominance[4]. Many of the early towns had also facilities for trade, either from their position on navigable rivers or the sea. It was

[1] *Growth*, I. 210.   [2] *Ibid.* I. 400.
[3] *Ibid.* I. 174, 215.   [4] *Ibid.* I. 215, 229.

the aim of the townsmen to make the most of these resources so that the town might continue to flourish, and that the trade in which they engaged should react on the prosperity of the town itself. They aimed at freedom to pursue their own economic prosperity, and this freedom seems to have been symbolised by the possession of a Guild Merchant. The townsmen had no authority to regulate affairs over an extended area[1], but they did their best to foster the prosperity of the place over which they had jurisdiction. From this it followed that in the Middle Ages there was a great development of municipal regulation and inter-municipal commerce; comparatively little attempt was made to survey the prosperity of the realm as a whole or to make the various places cooperate for the common weal. The towns were of course bound to make payments to the Crown, and they might be willing at times to agree to large payments for national purposes; still, their policy was not dictated by any national objects, but by the consideration of the needs of the town itself, or of those who lived in it.

[1] Power was given to the Scottish Merchant Guilds to exclusive commercial rights over a much larger area than in the case of English boroughs. *Scottish Historical Review*, L. 168.

(ii) *The Formation of Capital*

(24) In the mediaeval cities we can notice a stage when goods were hoarded. It is a step towards the formation of capital; the town authorities were concerned to see that there was an adequate corn supply, especially in cases where the corn was obtained by trade and was not the produce of home fields. The corn policy of the towns involved the hoarding of considerable stocks[1] which were sold to meet the requirements of the citizens, but it does not appear to have been pursued with the object of making an income by these transactions; and so these granaries are properly regarded as hoards and not as capital. There was need for a similar municipal policy in regard to fuel. London regulated the prices of billets and Dublin laid up a stock of coals. In the seventeenth century London became much more dependent on sea-borne coal from Newcastle than it had been in earlier times. The right to have a share in the stocks which the town laid up, must have been one of considerable importance; in later times the stock seems to have been sold at special rates for the good of the poor. But in early days we find that great importance was attached to membership of the Guild Merchant ; and though this institution is in many ways

[1] Ashley, *Introduction to Economic History*, I. ii. 33.

obscure, it seems, in such an English town as Shrewsbury, to have consisted of all the townsmen who were concerned in buying and selling, not merely of capitalists who made an income from trade[1]. Among the privileges which it offered was the right of cavel or sharing in the town purchases; this practice of buying of stock, to be subsequently shared, appears to have been maintained by many bodies throughout the Middle Ages; possibly with some of the religious guilds it came to be a form of investing capital which could be subsequently realised at a profit instead of lying idle.

We have not sufficient data to trace the beginnings of capital with any clearness; the accumulation of a hoard is the first stage, and the use of these hoards to obtain an income is a second stage. By far the larger number of craftsmen through the Middle Ages would hardly be conscious of any return on capital itself, but would have thought of their stock in trade as something to be constantly replenished so that they might be able to live by their work. It was by his work that a man lived; his stock in trade was subsidiary; the materials might often be supplied by the customer, as was the case both in the tailoring,

---

[1] *Growth*, I. 221. On the other hand the Merchant Guilds in Scotland were apparently composed of men engaged in trade. *Royal Hist. Soc. Trans.* 3rd Ser. VII. 4.

the building, and the goldsmith's trade; and it seems to have been in dealing in wares, that the capitalist began consciously to look for a profit on money expended and to be eager to realise his stock at a profit. This is as true of the petty dealer or pedlar who carries wares of many kinds in a pack, as of the shipman who ventures across the sea. A vast amount of the commerce of the Middle Ages was carried on at fairs; these institutions were frequented by foreigners[1] and were places where consumers had the best opportunities of purchasing goods, and there were abundant facilities for the enforcement of contracts and the recovery of debts. At the fair each buyer and seller was acting on his own account and influenced by pecuniary considerations; and the habit thus engendered survived in the conception of the freedom of the individual to buy and sell as he likes, a freedom which strongly asserted itself in James I's reign when monopolies and chartered companies were so much under discussion.

[1] The principle of restricting the alien was more successfully carried out in Scotland, where there do not appear to have been fairs which foreigners frequented, and where they were obliged to sell to native merchants at their place of landing (*Scottish Historical Review*, L. 170). But even in England, despite the large customs which alien merchants paid, and the favour with which they were regarded by the Crown, the townsmen were, on the whole, successful in restraining them from competing in the retail trade.

(25) The history of English towns in the thirteenth and fourteenth centuries is to a large extent
the story of a struggle against the encroachment of
the alien capitalist in internal trade, and especially
in trade within the towns themselves. Englishmen
of the thirteenth century could not pretend to any
considerable part, either in the export of native productions, or in the import of foreign wares[1]. Foreign
trade was entirely in the hands of aliens, especially
in those of the great Italian houses; but the townsmen
were anxious to keep the profits of retail trade
entirely in their own hands. The importers from
abroad were necessary as wholesale dealers, but there
seemed to be no occasion for them to compete in
retailing goods. With the townsmen this was not
wholly a question of opportunities of pecuniary gain,
but to some extent a question of principle, and of
facilities for enforcing a trade policy which was
favourable to the prosperity of the town; a social
and communal interest was recognised apart from
private gain, and public spirit had a real place in civic
regulation. The tradition of the subordination of
private interest to public welfare, which found expres-
sion in the regulation of mediaeval towns, survived
to become dominant on a larger scale, partly under

---

[1] *Growth*, I. 197, 628.

royal and partly under Parliamentary influence, in
the mercantile system.

In some of the economic regulations, which were
necessary for early town life, the towns had been
anticipated by the royal household and the monasteries. The royal purveyors had devised regulations
which were of importance for the purchaser and the
consumer; the assize of bread and beer and the regulation of weights and measures, might have been taken
over bodily by the towns. But the towns were not
merely interested in the consumption of wealth; the
prosperity of many of them depended on continued
production, and the regulation of industry occupied
much of their attention; the rules as to hours of work
and conditions for the maintenance of labour must
have already become traditional in the great monasteries and the armouries of mediaeval castles. Thus
the two chief phases of mediaeval regulation of
towns may possibly have been derived from the
social groups which they superseded.

The end of the fourteenth, and beginning of the
fifteenth century marked a further step of progress, as
Englishmen had become ambitious of competing with
the alien in foreign trade. In the time of Edward III
Parliament had been content that English wool should
be shipped abroad in foreign bottoms[1], and that

---

[1] *Growth*, I. 415.

imports should be brought by foreign fleets; but
in the subsequent reigns there was a change, and
deliberate efforts were made to encourage English
shipping at the expense of foreigners. The founding
of the Merchant Adventurers marks one stage in
the progress; and the rise of great ship-owners, like
William Canynges[1] shows that there were English
capitalists who were ready to take advantage of their
opportunities. The Venetian galleys ceased to visit
England in the early sixteenth century, and the trade
was eventually taken up by the Turkey Company.
The struggle with German rivals was long and em-
bittered; the Hanseatic League obtained a new status
under Edward IV[2], and it was not till the reign of
Elizabeth that they were really ousted from their
importance in the carrying trade, and that the foreign
trade of England came to be done in English ships.

(iii) *Capitalism and the Organisation of Industry*

(26) Each of the master craftsmen in an
ordinary mediaeval town was in a sort of way a capitalist; he catered for the wants of the public in a
market, and by the sale of his wares got the means for
buying materials and providing tools to carry on his
work. But the organisation of industry was not

[1] *Growth*, I. 387.
[2] Ian D. Colvin, *The Germans in England*, pp. 117 f.

capitalistic: each craftsman was generally speaking his own employer, and did not depend on any one else for the requisites of production. The distinguishing feature of the capitalist organisation of industry is the possession of the materials by the employer, who engages the workman and pays his wages; he subsequently makes a profit by the sale of the goods, and it may be convenient that he should provide the place of work and the implements of work, as well as the materials. The intrusion of capital may not make much apparent change in the conditions under which work is done, but it makes a tremendous change in the personal relations of the workman to his fellow men when he is reduced to a position of dependence.

The craftsman who works on the domestic system[1] is independent, but his methods and hours of work

[1] This term is used in the sense in which it was current in Yorkshire at the beginning of the nineteenth century (*Reports*, 1806, III. 1058). Mr G. Unwin (*Industrial Organisation*, p. 4) defines the terms quite differently and opposes the guild to the domestic system, as separate and successive phases of development; but this does not seem to me to apply to English history. I prefer to say that the domestic system existed from the earliest times, but that it has been gradually superseded by capitalism, and that the craft guild was a form of regulation which was appropriate to the domestic system. Some of the fifteenth century London companies were capitalist in character and so, generally speaking, were the seventeenth century companies. Trade Unions as associations of wage-earners testify by their very existence to the severance of classes, which is partly the cause and partly the effect of capitalistic organisation.

need not be unregulated: the craft guilds afforded a
method of mutual supervision by the good men of
the trade.

The origin of craft guilds, like other origins, is
obscure, it may even have been anticipated by the
organisation of dependents near castles or monasteries.
It is quite possible that in Italy and France a practice
which was widely extended in the Roman Empire
survived in mediaeval times; but though there is
much room for difference of opinion as to the origin
of craft guilds, there is ample evidence as to their
character and powers. In England the craft guild
appears to have been an institution which obtained
powers from the town to regulate a certain industry
for the common good[1]. On its economic side it
aimed at supplying a known market, by meeting
the wants of the townsmen themselves and of others
who visited it for the purpose of buying; it strove,
besides, to maintain a high quality of wares, the good
training of the workmen, and favourable conditions
for work; but the whole institution was subordinated
to the good of the town, and to the steady growth of
a material prosperity in which all could share. The
mayor and public authorities were quite ready to
disallow any ordinances which seemed to be in the
selfish interest of a trade and inconsistent with the

[1] *Growth*, I. 338.

welfare of the community. The craftsman who had served an apprenticeship obtained a status in London, and the system was more important because of the social status it conferred in the life of the town than because of the technical training it provided. But the system was not so hard and fast as is sometimes supposed, for the London citizen was free to work at any calling whether he had been apprenticed to it or not[1], so long as he kept to the rules that regulated that calling.

The whole of this system served admirably for the regulation of industry under suitable conditions, but it made no allowance for growth; and in the fourteenth and fifteenth centuries there appears to have been a rapid growth, especially in connection with the manufacture of cloth for distant markets. Those who, as dealers, had formed some capital and were accustomed to handle it, began to invest their capital in industry and to compete with those who were craftsmen by training. The dealers might be dealers in raw material, or dealers in the finished product; but in either case they did not count to make an income by their own work, but by the wealth they had invested in buying materials and tools and used for paying wages. The capitalist system in the cloth trade appears to be as old as the incursion of Flemish

[1] *Growth*, I. 345.

weavers under Edward III, and it certainly had reached a high stage of development in the sixteenth century, when men like Jack of Winchcomb and Stump of Marlborough flourished[1]. These men did not manufacture with reference to a market on the spot, but with reference to the requirements of a distant market, sometimes a market in foreign countries. They had an interest in manufacturing on as large a scale as possible, and turning over their capital rapidly so as to enable them to push their trade and get the command of a larger market[2]. It is obvious that institutions which were built up by small craftsmen, each with his stock in trade, to meet a known market were unsuited to the industry as developed by large capitalists. The regulations, which had been maintained in the old corporate towns, were proving inconvenient in the fifteenth century, and industries migrated from the towns to the rural districts. In other cases the burden of taxation appears to have been oppressive to the old communities, while it is likely enough that some of them had never recovered from the ravages of the Black Death. At any rate

[1] *Growth*, I. 523.

[2] Mr R. H. Tawney has made an excellent point by showing that in the cloth manufacture the wages authoritatively fixed were a minimum, not as in most employments a maximum. *Vierteljahrsschrift für Social- und Wirthschaftliche Geschichte*, XI. 542.

we see that, in the middle of the sixteenth century, the institutions, which had served to regulate the industry of the towns in the Middle Ages, were no longer effective for their purpose.

(27) The towns thus lost their importance as organised centres of economic life[1] and they also ceased to be regarded as important units for political purposes[2]. There had been a time when the payments that they made, for the enjoyment of self-government, and occasionally to meet special demands, were of great importance to the Crown, and the maintenance of the prosperity of each town was a matter of public concern; this feeling prevailed as late as the time of Philip and Mary; but it appears that from that time onwards governmental measures were rather directed to fostering the prosperity of the realm as a whole than to maintaining the economic activity of particular towns. But during

[1] The Scottish towns had very little organisation for industrial purposes till the eve of the Reformation, and their municipal life was not so highly developed as that of England. The Scottish boroughs pursued a policy which was laid down for all by the Convention of Boroughs, and do not appear to have been so particularised as English towns.

[2] The early part of the seventeenth century appears to have been the time when the common good of the Scottish boroughs began to be much mismanaged by grants in severalty on terms which were advantageous to individuals, but injurious to the town in the long run.

the seventeenth century old payments[1] had, with the alteration of the value of money, become almost nominal and had often been redeemed. The town privileges of self government had ceased to give substantial advantages; the capitalists, who had settled in suburbs or in the country, were developing a profitable business; the joint stock companies gave increased opportunity in the investment of capital on lines which lay outside municipal authority; by 1689 the towns were no longer seeking so much to preserve an independent life of their own, but were more content to have their share in the general prosperity of the country.

In the present century there has been a certain revival of town life, but this revival has been directed and controlled by national authority. New duties of many sorts have been undertaken by municipalities in connection with lighting, sanitation, education and other matters; and this has brought about a greatly increased burden on the rates. There have also been many schemes of municipal trading especially in public services, such as the supply of gas and water. For many of these public works a town has found it necessary to rely on its credit and borrow the capital it requires, but in all matters of economic management the State overhauls municipal

[1] Webb, *English Local Government*, II. 287.

affairs and determines the conditions and period for
which loans may be raised. Municipal public spirit
and revived civic patriotism have done much for the
welfare of urban populations, but there has been no
tendency to revive the particularism of mediaeval
towns or to break up the solidarity of the nation.

PART III. THE DIRECTION AND CONTROL OF
PRIVATE CAPITAL THROUGHOUT THE COUNTRY

(i) *The Resources of the Country as a whole*

(28) The beginning of the reign of Elizabeth, when
Burghley came into power, marks a great turning point
in the economic history of England; since this was
the beginning of an endeavour to treat the whole
realm as a unit for economic purposes and to organise
and stimulate the economic activities of the nation.
It was a limited area that the household controlled; the
cities of the Middle Ages had not an extended jurisdiction, though the influence of the custom of London
and of some other ancient cities was felt in many
towns; but in the Tudor times the Royal Council was
sufficiently in touch with all parts of the country to
attempt to control the economic conditions in every
district, and to frame all the arrangements on one
model. This would hardly have been attempted

unless a time of disintegration had intervened, when the old manorial system had broken up and many of the old corporate towns decayed. The social organisms of the past were ready to be superseded in Tudor times; and the royal administration made vigorous efforts to supersede them effectively.

The solidarity of the realm, which is noticeable from Tudor times onwards, is chiefly due to the fact that the government had come to derive its main income not from private estates but from public taxation. The development of agriculture had provided a fund from which subsidies, and later the land tax, could be drawn; while the increase of commerce had brought about the possibility of collecting a large revenue from customs. The interest of the government thus came to be bound up in the prosperity of the community as it had never been before. A great constitutional struggle was waged over the question whether the national interest, of the government and the governed, should be controlled in the last resort by the Crown, or by the representatives of the people; and this was practically settled by the issue of the Civil War. It is far more difficult to trace the steps by which the administration was adapted to modern conditions, and organised departments took the place of personal officials[1]. But the organisation of the

[1] The customers of mediaeval times had a very free hand,

Economic Activities of the country has gradually been brought under popular control, both as regards the policy to be pursued, and the machinery by which it is to be put into effect. Since Elizabethan times there has been no retrogression; the nation is the unit of economic life, and there has been an increase in the solidarity of the realm. The personal monarchy has passed away, and the administration is no longer confined to the king and his advisers; Parliament has come to the front as the body which shapes the economic policy of the country, by Navigation laws, Corn Bounty laws, and such like enactments which have been subsequently repealed by the authority which framed them. Commissions of enquiry and commissioners with executive powers have been created to deal with local or subsidiary matters, but the realm has been treated as a whole; and it has no longer been possible for one municipality to aim at making regulations which it could enforce so as to hurt the trade of another.

but were brought more and more under the supervision of the Exchequer. Recourse was had very frequently to the alternative system of farming the customs, but the farmers were suspected of serious frauds. Mr Hubert Hall has called my attention to a paper of 1641, which describes some of the malpractices by which there was a loss of revenue. After the Civil War, there was no great improvement till 1671, when a new board reinforced by new officials was constituted. From that time onwards the Customs became a true Revenue Department, and a branch of State finance under the Treasury.

National organisation may be contrasted on the economic side with the institutions which preceded it. It assumes the existence of capitalists, both in agriculture and industry. Subsistence farming was not yet extinct when national control was beginning to make itself felt; but much of the tillage of the country was carried on by men who worked for a market, and who were employers of labour; the same was true of the economic conditions which held good in the old corporate towns, as well as in the new districts into which manufacturing had spread. Everywhere the main responsibility for the economic life of the country lay in the hands of private capitalists; and the problem of any government, which desired to devise a system for the whole realm, was that of controlling and directing private capitalists[1]. It is on this account that we may feel in the Elizabethan era that we are at last in sight of modern habits of thought and modern problems; the age of invention gave us immensely increased power over the mechanical forces, but it did not introduce much that was wholly new in regard to personal relationships. The scale on which business was conducted in Elizabethan times was different from that with which we are familiar, it was mostly in

[1] In Scotland encouragement was given to private capitalists, and there was little attempt to control them. *Christianity and Politics*, p. 80.

the hands of quite small men. The wealthy capitalist
was exceptional; the combination of many industrial
capitalists into one great association with a joint stock
was only beginning[1]. But despite these differences
the practical problems of extending the market, and
the disputes between capital and labour, were similar
to those which have recently taken such gigantic proportions. There is no need to try and trace the course
of events in any particular industry, it will suffice to
offer a few illustrations of the changes.

(29) The aim of Lord Burghley, in devising a
national policy, appears to have been that of making
the most of the economic resources of the realm as a
whole. He was wonderfully successful in reducing
the waste which had come to be so generally current
in the fifteenth century. This aim was doubtless
strengthened by the political ambitions of Englishmen
to hold their own against continental powers and to
make a mark in the world. Tentative efforts to
check this or that abuse, and to introduce this or that
improvement may be noticed before this time, but it
is under Lord Burghley that systematic attention is
given to all the resources of the realm and their
development.

[1] An excellent account of early joint stock companies, in
extractive and other industries, is given by Prof. Scott, *The
Constitution and Finance of English, Scottish and Irish Joint
Stock Companies*, II. 383.

The rural districts were taken in hand by the Statute of the fifth of Elizabeth which regulated the conditions of agricultural labourers who were to be hired by the year. The previous regulations for wages had been definitely intended to fix a parliamentary maximum, but the Elizabethan machinery was more flexible, as it gave scope for the justices to assess the rates according to the plenty or scarcity of the time[1]. There was in this enactment a definite endeavour to do the fair thing for the community as a whole, and to do away with the excuse of the depopulators that they could not get labour for reasonable rates, as well as to remove the ground for the servants' complaint that they could not get reasonable wages. The organisation of the work of the household lay at the background of this national scheme, though the form which it took was suited to a capitalist society and a money economy. Besides this, every effort was made to improve the facilities for the sale of corn. It appears that the internal corn trade had suffered from the decay attending facilities of communication, both by road and water, during the fourteenth century. But in the sixteenth century there seems to have been a great revival of the internal corn trade[2]. The middlemen in this trade were under careful regulation, and the interests of the local poor, in getting their food

[1] *Growth*, II. 39.   [2] *Ibid.* II. 195.

cheap, appear to have been regarded; but the regulations for the corn bodgers and for the clerks of the
market show how widespread market institutions had
become. The need for supplying London drew agriculturists, at some distance from the metropolis, into
the circle of commerce; and it is evident that farm
produce other than corn was becoming more regularly
marketable. The great fairs of the Middle Ages had
for the most part been frequented by the dealers in
imported goods and those who wished to buy from
them; and these fairs appear to have declined, while
London increased in importance as a depot for foreign
goods; but from the beginning of the fifteenth century
onwards we hear of the multiplication of other fairs
at which cattle or horses were offered for sale. Some
of these fairs obtained a new importance by being
utilised as the opportunities for hiring labour, and of
making arrangements for the agricultural economy of
the year.

In the Middle Ages wool and wool-fells and hides
were the only articles of rural production which were
regularly exported, but in Elizabeth's reign account
was taken of an export trade in corn as well. From
the time of Elizabeth onwards there was an increasing
tendency to give encouragement to growers at home
by offering facilities for exportation, and this policy
culminated in the Corn Bounty Act of William and

Mary[1]. It seems probable that the government aimed at competing with the men of Zeeland and the Hanse Towns[2], who carried on a lucrative trade in supplying the Iberian Peninsula and Mediterranean lands with Baltic corn. However this may be, it is clear that from the reign of Elizabeth onwards there was an increasing market both at home and abroad for agricultural produce.

The development of agricultural resources led also to a considerable amount of permanent improvement, as in the draining of the fens, and to the plantations of sparsely inhabited districts within the realm. King James had been interested in the adventures of the Gentlemen of Fife who endeavoured to migrate to the island of Lewis[3], as well as in the attempts to settle the Grahams in Connaught[4] and the MacDonnells in Antrim[5], before the great scheme for the plantation of Ulster[6] was devised and carried through with the help of the London Companies. These experiments at home prepared the way for the more extensive undertakings which had the definite political

[1] There was an experiment in this direction under Charles II; 25 C. II. c. 1, § 31, Gras, *Quarterly Journal of Economics*, XXIV. 419.

[2] *Growth*, II. 87.

[3] Æ. Mackay, *Fife and Kinross*, 105.

[4] G. Hill, *Plantation of Ulster*, p. 228 n.

[5] G. Hill, *Macdonnells of Antrim*, p. 207.   [6] *Growth*, II. 362.

aim of establishing a counterpoise to Spain. In the New World, the English settlements in Virginia, the West Indies, and the North American coast were definitely plantations to which settlers went with the purpose of raising products from the soil. The Dutch were chiefly concerned in establishing commerce, while the main motive of the Spaniards appears to have been the prosecution of mining. But the character of the English settlements, as an extension of English soil inhabited by Englishmen, is sufficiently marked by the term, which was habitually applied to them, of plantations. The political problem, which was to emerge at a later date, had to do with the question of continuing to treat them as plantations, and as subsidiary to the country to which they were adjuncts, or of recognising their claims to an independent life of their own.

Burghley also made systematic efforts to remedy neglect with regard to the mineral wealth of England; something had been done in the Middle Ages in mining for silver and the lead with which it was frequently associated. But Burghley was actively interested in reviving or re-introducing metallurgical industries and in working up useful metals, especially those which were necessary for providing ordnance and munitions[1].

[1] *Growth*, II. 58.

Keswick, Somersetshire, and Monmouthshire, were the
scenes of mining operations; and it is clear enough
that an extensive mining industry was beginning.
Though the fuel employed in the iron smelting in the
Forest of Dean and the Sussex Weald was wood, coal
mining received a certain impulse from the increased
dependence on this form of fuel for domestic purposes,
and more capital was sunk in pumps for coal mines
during the seventeenth century than in almost any
other industrial mechanism[1].

Burghley was not only concerned to make the
most of the land itself but he also interested himself
in the harvest of the sea; it was his main project to
encourage the fishing trade by insisting upon an increased consumption of fish. The keeping of fish days[2]
had been in vogue on religious grounds before the
Reformation, and Cecil desired to see the old practice
maintained with increased rigour. The fishing trades
were a school of seamanship, the political importance
of having mariners who could defend the realm was
recognised, and the interests of commerce were also
borne in mind; but the economic character of fishing,
as both giving employment and adding to the food
supply, marked it out as an industry to be specially
encouraged. The subsidiary employments in the

---

[1] *Growth*, II. 529.   [2] *Ibid.* II. 68.

preservation of wood for shipbuilding[1] and the supply
of hemp and sailcloth engaged attention, and pains
were also taken in making enquiries as to the state
of havens[2] and devising means for the improvement
of them[3].

Besides attending to the organising of existing
industries Burghley also encouraged the planting of
new employments. There was a long standing tradition as to the wealth which had been brought to the
country by foreign artisans in the time of Henry I
and again under Edward III. Steps were taken to
encourage the settlement of foreign weavers in the
eastern counties, at Stamford and elsewhere. The
fulling mill at Colchester and the ancient factory at
Dedham are monuments of a new development which
was not always very welcome at the time, but which
proved highly beneficial in the long run. The industrial impulse that was given at this time was not
confined to urban districts but came to be widely
diffused throughout the counties where weaving was
taken up by some of the men; spinning offered a
remunerative occupation to women and children.

---

[1] *Growth*, II. 64.   [2] *Ibid*. II. 66.
[3] It is noticeable that the settlement of Newfoundland,
which was one of our earliest colonies, was undertaken with
a view to developing the fishing industry there far more than
with any intention of planting.

It seems to have been in the latter part of the sixteenth century that spinning came to be diffused so widely in many of the counties of England as to form an important by-occupation, the loss of which was seriously felt at the time of the industrial revolution[1].

The planting of these manufactures was one of the efforts which were made for dealing with the social problems of unemployment. In the period of Edward VI and the early years of Elizabeth this problem had reached enormous proportions; it was a period of transition; the increase of sheep farming doubtless led to the eviction of some of the peasantry and the progress of agriculture tended towards the impoverishment of others. Attempts to induce the vagrant population to settle on the wastes were a somewhat doubtful expedient, but the providing of facilities for work and training in new forms of work was an undoubted boon. Parishes were encouraged to buy a stock of wool or flax by which they could set the poor on work and this seems to have been a more successful method of relieving poverty than the granting of

[1] In the eighteenth and nineteenth centuries we hear a good deal of the improving landlords in Scotland who introduced by-occupations of different kinds into their villages. This had probably been accomplished at an earlier period in England and in the eighteenth century manufacturing was a subsidiary occupation in many districts though in some counties it was little developed.

relief by the overseers. To whatever cause it may have been due it appears that the Elizabethan system was at last successful in restraining pauperism within the limits in which it was possible to deal with it effectively[1]. And in the early part of the seventeenth century England appears to have been extraordinarily well organised as a realm, both as regards the conditions of employment and the maintenance of the unemployed.

Similar undertakings were being pushed on with great rapidity in France where Henry IV was taking active measures for the improvement of the prosperity of a realm that had suffered terribly from long continued wars. In France the initiative came chiefly from the Crown or the royal officers; and many public works, especially for internal communication, were undertaken at public expense. The English Crown was not able to carry out improvements in this way, but endeavoured to enlist the co-operation of subjects by appealing to their sense of duty, or by holding out hopes of ultimate pecuniary reward. It was by such means that the City Companies were induced to undertake the planting of Ulster, and that adventurers were found to sink their wealth in the draining of the fens. Because the improvements were introduced incidentally, there was never the same systematic government

[1] Leonard, *Early History of English Poor Relief*, p. 21.

organisation as has been generally accepted in France, while on the other hand the ultimate gain accruing from these improvements has passed very largely into the private hands of the heirs of those who co-operated in the adventure. There has never been a great bureaucracy in this country, as statesmen have for the most part been content to direct and control the employment of private capital.

The corporate towns had evidently fallen on evil days and we hear of many complaints with regard to their decay in the time of Henry VIII and of Philip and Mary. The guilds which had been the main instruments of regulating industry were attacked on their religious side, and forfeited such of their property, together with trust property, as was devoted to religious objects; and it appears that their industrial activities were for the most part superseded. Measures very similar to those which they had enjoined in regard to the production of wares, for the good of the reputation of a town, were now enacted by parliamentary authority for the whole of the realm. The custom of London with regard to the training of apprentices for many callings during the long period of seven years was now in force throughout the country[1]; and the arrangements with regard to the conditions of apprenticeship and the payment of labourers became

---

[1] *Growth*, II. 30.

a matter of national, not merely of local significance.
The local companies, even though their main economic
functions were undertaken by national authorities, did
not always die out. In not a few cases they were
restored or re-established by royal authority or by act
of Parliament[1], but this revival seems on the whole
to have been due to a desire to discriminate against
aliens, sometimes against foreign Protestants and
sometimes against Scots. The municipal companies
do not seem to have played an active part in
the regulation of industry or to have made a
serious resistance to the encroachment of national
organisation.

(30) Further evidence of the solidarity of the realm
is afforded by the increased reliance of the government
on taxation. The Crown could not be well off unless
the community were prospering; the interests of the
Crown and the subjects were more at one. During
the Middle Ages the king had lived " of his own "; the
management of the Crown estates had little to do
with the public at large, and Parliament was called
upon to supplement the necessities of the king, not as
a regular rule but on special occasions. In modern
times, when the realm is considered as a whole,
the expenses of government have ceased to be a

---

[1] *Growth,* II. 37.

distinct item contributed out of special resources, but have been merged in the other charges on the economic activities of the country. The defence of the realm by land or by sea, and the expenses of police and internal government, are on the whole defrayed by means of taxation. As soon as taxation came to be the main resource on which the government relied, a constitutional demand arose on the part of those, who contributed to the expenses, for the control of the government. The struggle during the reign of Charles I was a mark of the new dependence of the Crown on revenue collected from the people, and therefore on popular support. The government had been accustomed to avoid direct appeals for support on particular issues by means of borrowing. Capitalist classes had met the necessities of the Crown under Edward III as well as in the beginning of the seventeenth century. The turning point in this matter came in the time of Charles I when he found himself unable to borrow in the city without associating Parliament with himself to give security to his creditors[1]. He was thus forced to assent to the measure which deprived him of the power of dissolving the Long Parliament; and popular consent was required, not only for the granting of taxation, which was chiefly drawn from the landed classes, but also

[1] *Growth*, II. 411.

for temporary accommodation from the monied men as well. It was thus that the Crown ceased to be an independent economic interest within the realm, and that the expenses of government came to be the concern of the public at large. The change thus effected had a decided effect on the economic administration of the realm; taxes could be most easily collected from the landed classes, and as a consequence it became a matter of administrative importance that rents should be high. It was also desirable that trade should expand so that Customs duties might be considerable; while direct dealings with the monied classes developed and became a matter of not only occasional help but of permanent assistance.

(ii) *Relations to other Countries*

(31) The attempt to view the realm as one economic whole brought into clearer light the question of the relations of the English realm to other realms. Mediaeval regulation, like mediaeval commerce, had been to a large extent intermunicipal, concerning the trade between particular places or the trade in commodities. These were now to be merged in the consideration of the trade of the country as a whole; this meant as a practical thing that the trade of London came more to the front[1], and that of the

[1] The great regulated and joint stock companies were mostly London companies; on the relations with out ports see

out ports relatively declined; but both the Crown and Parliament were endeavouring to aim at measures which would benefit the whole, and in the early seventeenth century they had shown little favour for the abnormal growth of the great city at the mouth of the Thames[1].

Burghley had no doubts about the benefit which accrued from promoting the material prosperity of the country and its shores; but the question was more complicated in regard to foreign commerce. In the Middle Ages, and in the sixteenth century, the ordinary articles of export and import had a very different character from the exports and imports of this country in the present day. The exports were for the most part materials which could be used in industry, such as wool and hides or useful metals, such as lead and tin. There was comparatively little benefit to the community in supplying these things to foreigners instead of getting the good of them at home. On the other hand the imported goods consisted chiefly of fine manufactures, and wines; they were articles of luxury, and it had been the interest of the Court and the wealthy that they

Miss M. Sellers, *Merchant Adventurers of Newcastle*; a great deal of evidence in regard to West Country trade, in the latter part of Elizabeth's reign, is given in a document printed by Gras, *Development of English Corn Trade*, App. J. p. 429.

[1] *Growth*, II. 311.

should be plentiful and cheap, as was seen especially in the time of Edward III. But the diffusion of these things at cheap rates among the people did not make for the prosperity of the country in the long run. In this way it was possible to identify exportation with the sale of raw materials which might be manufactured at home, and importation with luxurious expenditure. Burghley was not inclined to give much encouragement to foreign commerce as such; there was need for discrimination[1]. Foreign commerce seemed to him an evil, in so far as it increased luxury, but he regarded it as beneficial in so far as it gave a vent for English commodities and therefore an encouragement to economic activities at home. Exploration and discovery which opened up new markets, were very beneficial from his point of view; but frequent communication with countries that were more advanced than ourselves was not a thing to be regarded with enthusiasm. Commerce has been the means of initiating the progress of industries and the growth of capitalism. Burghley was not a sentimentalist who regarded material progress as a bad thing[2]; but he was anxious that the steps in material progress should be really used in such a way as to contribute to the prosperity of the

---

[1] *Growth*, II. 71.

[2] Reactionaries who idealise a country in a stationary state, like China, give little help in guiding material progress wisely, so as to get rid of its incidental evils.

realm, and not merely for the benefit of individuals; and still more that material progress should not cause disadvantage to any portion of the community.

At that time it seemed possible to take a rough and ready index which served to show whether the effect of any branch of commerce was beneficial to the community or not. If the value of the commodities exported to any country exceeded the value of the commodities imported from that country, there was a balance to be paid by that country in bullion. This bullion, whether hoarded by the Crown as treasure or invested as capital, was a gain to the country as a whole; and in this way the balance of trade was taken as an index for distinguishing hurtful from profitable commerce. This doctrine, which was clearly stated by Lord Burghley, dominated English policy in regard to foreign trade during the seventeenth and eighteenth centuries[1], though it underwent some modification; it shows us the main motive which underlay the special jealousy of the French trade which is so noticeable in the period after the Restoration and in the eighteenth century.

(32) Though the benefit of foreign commerce was a matter of debate, there was a general agreement as to the importance of maintaining English shipping.

---

[1] *Growth*, II. 395.

The parliament of Edward III had been quite content
that foreign trade should be carried on by foreigners
and that they should bear the risks of loss and piracy
at sea. But Englishmen of the sixteenth century
were inclined to make light of these risks, and to
regard English shipping as of prime importance for
the prosperity of an island realm. The coasts suffered
from the raids of pirates, whether from the north of
Europe or, as in the time of Charles I, from Algerians[1].
Ships were the best defence against such raiders, or
against any threatened invasion from France or
Flanders. Whatever rendered shipping plentiful gave
facilities for repelling invasion and attacking foes,
and from these political motives the development of
shipping came to be recognised as an element of
supreme importance in the economic policy of the
realm. The good and evil of various methods for
encouraging shipping was a matter of dispute. The
policy of granting special concessions to the owners
of ships engaged in particular trades was much
criticised in the time of James I; but the policy of
confining English trade to English ships, which had
been fitfully tried from the fourteenth century
onwards, was deliberately adopted in the time of the
Council of State[2] and persistently maintained by
subsequent parliaments.

[1] *Growth*, II 173.   [2] *Ibid.* II. 359.

(iii) *The Monied Interest*

(33) The eighteenth century was marked by the continuance of the scheme of national policy which had been devised at the time of Elizabeth, but it showed some very marked differences.   In Elizabeth's time the Crown had obtained extraordinary power and prestige, and the whole administration in regard to economic conditions was in the hands of royal officials and representatives.   But the Civil War made an extraordinary difference in diminishing the effectiveness of royal power; Parliamentary claims to authority were practically admitted during the Restoration Period, and came to be patently acknowledged from the time of the Revolution onwards. It is even more striking that while the Elizabethan regulation was primarily concerned with land and employment, in the eighteenth century the question of external trade, which was in the hands of the monied interest, seemed to dominate other sides of national life.

In the eighteenth century the special problems of rural disintegration and depopulation were not so prominent as in the sixteenth[1], and the Corn Bounty Act appeared to give a regular and sufficient market for corn.   We hear comparatively little of disputes

[1] See p. 52, above.

about wages, possibly because so many men had some
independent source of income, and received wages as
a by-occupation[1]. The machinery which had been
established for the settlement of wages seems to have
been in operation after the Civil War[2], but at the end
of the eighteenth century it appears to have been
practically forgotten. Nor were there fresh legislative
experiments about the provision for the unemployed.
The Act of Charles II, by defining the places at which
any individual had the right of demanding relief[3],
interfered seriously with the fluidity of labour and
gave occasion for much costly legislation. There was
no uniformity in the administration of relief throughout the realm, and the differences of local custom
were an obstacle to any general improvement on the
Elizabethan system. The progress of enclosing and
of agricultural improvement was going on slowly
but steadily, and this was apt to tell against the
stability of the labourers' position; though these
changes improved the pecuniary position of the land
owners relatively to their neighbours, they were losing
their exclusive influence in the affairs of State.

On the other hand the improvement of another
side of economic activity was coming more and more

---

[1] R. H. Tawney, *Vierteljahrsschrift für Social- una Wirthschaftliche Geschichte*, XI. 537.

[2] *Ibid.* XI. 327.   [3] *Growth*, II. 570.

to the front; we hear much, in the seventeenth and eighteenth centuries, of the political importance of the monied men and they came to be a much more striking factor than formerly in economic life. The foundation of the Bank of England, and of the numerous Provincial Banks which followed its lead, gave an immense impulse to the forming of capital. We see in the stories of men like Pepys how difficult it had been for private persons to know what to do with their hoards[1]. But the Bank of England enabled the private person to obtain an interest on his money while the money could be still more remuneratively employed in loans to government or to private persons who were in need of capital. By opening up opportunities for obtaining an income, the eighteenth century did a very great deal for the investment of hoards as capital. Still greater prominence came to the owners of capital through the recognition of the power of credit. By means of its credit the government was able to obtain funds to be used for special emergencies. By means of their credit, as the recipients of a large income from government, the Bank of England was able to obtain command of large sums of money, and lend them to those who had the prospects of trading successfully; and hence during the

[1] *Diary of Samuel Pepys*, 12 Nov. 1666, 13 and 19 June 1667, and 10 Oct. 1667.

eighteenth century the practice of borrowing money
to meet emergencies and of trading on borrowed
capital came to be general, not only by merchants
and manufacturers, but by agriculturists as well.
The question of the direction of this capital into the
most profitable channels, so that the country might
prosper as much as possible, was the main economic
problem of the eighteenth century in England.

(34) It seemed to the men of the time as if the
whole of the varied prosperity of the country could be
summed up under one formula and gauged by means
of the balance of trade[1]. Activity in the improvement of land or breeding of cattle would give larger
produce to be exported and would therefore result in
a more favourable balance of trade. Similarly the
increase of manufacturing, which enabled us to
dispense with goods of foreign production or to
compete with more success in outside markets, would
diminish imports and increase exports and thus bring
about a more favourable balance of trade. A study
of the balance, and the encouragement of trades which
contributed largely to the balance, and the discourage-
ment of others which showed an unfavourable balance
was the constant study of economists and financiers.
But as time went on it came to be apparent that this

[1] *Growth*, II. 396.

criterion was not really reliable, and that legislators were not justified in following it blindly. The result was much confused by the possibilities of three-cornered trade; it was also affected by the movements of capital for investment in any country or by loans to government. As early as the beginning of the seventeenth century it had been pointed out that the export of a little treasure to India might bring about the importation of quantities of goods which could be sold in Europe so as to bring in a far larger quantity of bullion than had been originally exported[1]. It was not, however, till the *Wealth of Nations* was published that the British public came to recognise that the balance of trade was illusory as a criterion of the national gain to be derived from different trades. Adam Smith endeavoured to restate the doctrine and discriminated the advantage of employing capital in one way or another according to the amount of labour it set in motion. But this criterion was cumbrous; and on the whole the public were content to believe that it was unnecessary to look behind private gain, and that capital that was employed for a profit to the owner was somehow or other beneficial to the public.

(35) Partly on practical grounds of administrative difficulty in enforcing them, and partly

[1] *Growth*, II. 257.

because of uncertainty about the aim which should be kept in view, the nationalist regulations for agriculture, industry and commerce fell into discredit and found few defenders.

The fifteenth century, when manorial and municipal institutions were disintegrating and decaying, appears to have been a time of increasing poverty, apart from the advance of the cloth trade; but the eighteenth century was a time of more general advance, and the system of regulation, which was falling into decay, could be represented as hampering rather than favouring progress on the line which it was now taking. The commercial companies, which had been organised to carry on trade that should react favourably on industrial life at home had been discredited as interfering with the most energetic traders; the interlopers had on the whole won the day; and joint stock companies, with their large capital, had triumphed over the associations of smaller men who dealt as members of regulated companies. In industry, too, there was a tendency to organise on a large scale which rendered division of labour more possible; while the improved implements and machines were adding to the importance of the capitalist factor in manufacturing, and the labourer was being reduced to a position of greater dependence. Even in agriculture, the capitalist, who worked for foreign markets, could afford to pay a higher rent than the yeoman class who maintained the traditional subsistence farming. While on the one side we see increased facilities for the formation and investment of capital, on the other everything was tending to give greater prominence to capital as an element in national prosperity; and there seemed to be sufficient justification for assuming that if the capitalists were gaining, the affairs of the country were prospering as well.

During the last quarter of the eighteenth century a doubt began to arise in men's minds as to whether it was ever worth while to take account of the wealth of the nation as a political unit, or whether there was any ground for distinguishing it from the wealth of the private persons who composed the State at any given time. Private persons who prospered could be counted upon to contribute to the expense of the State in whatever way they made their money. After the independence of the American colonists had been secured, when it was found that trade with the American plantations was as profitable as it had been before, the whole colonial system was called in question; Sir John Sinclair and others bitterly inveighed against the policy of extending our territory[1]. When the land of the country and the development of landed resources had been the chief consideration,

[1] *Growth*, II. 850.

there seemed to be little doubt about the advantage of extending possessions abroad and of resources which the nation could control. But when the nation lost control economically over the plantations, and it was found that in their political independence they afforded a good market for English goods and supplied commodities of which England had need, the question assumed a different shape. The victory of Trafalgar, and the consequent establishing of the unrivalled maritime power of Britain, seemed to render it unnecessary to pay any special attention to the political aspects of national wealth or to raise any question as to what trades were good for the community. All ground for interference on the part of the State with the manner in which a man employed his capital seemed to be taken away, and when the nineteenth century opened public opinion was inclined to leave the capitalist perfectly free to employ his wealth in any enterprise he chose, and to regard the profit which he secured as the best proof that his enterprise was beneficial to the State. This had been the view which was practically adopted by Scotsmen from the beginning of the seventeenth century, and it was now accepted in England as well.

(iv)   *Laissez Faire*

(36)   There were remarkable contrasts between
the opening of the seventeenth and of the nineteenth
centuries not only in the enormously increased amount
and power of capital, but in the attitude towards it
which was taken by public opinion and the State.
Capitalism in the seventeenth century was suspected
as a power which might be used merely in private
interests, unless it was directed authoritatively towards
public purposes.   The public purposes might be political, such as the encouragement of shipping with a
view to the defence of the coast; or they might be
social in keeping a watch on capitalism and pro-
tecting the weak from the strong and the poor from
the rich.   But things had so far changed that the
public, in the early nineteenth century, were inclined to
accept capitalism as in itself sufficient and satisfactory
for public purposes.   There seemed to be no need to
direct it; and if there were no need, any direction,
which necessarily involved restriction, was hurtful.
The capitalist was regarded as the enterprising person
who saw what was best for his own business and who
necessarily took the course that favoured the most
rapid progress of the nation.   In the early nineteenth
century it was clear that material progress was a good
thing, that it opened up possibilities for welfare of

every kind both for individuals and for the nation, and the high rate of profit, which stimulated private enterprise, was generally taken as a criterion of national prosperity[1].

It thus came about that the public were inclined to trust to the private capitalist for the organisation of economic activities on the best possible lines; and during the first half of the nineteenth century the provisions which had been made for economic objects of national importance were ruthlessly swept away without any attempt to supply a substitute.

(*a*) The great industrial code which had been established during the reign of Elizabeth to secure the good training of workmen, was abolished. The seven years' apprenticeship was proving unnecessarily long; in certain cases, it interfered with the rapid expansion of some of the textile trades, and during the wars a strain was put upon it which seemed to involve a temporary suspension in order to avoid injustice to good workmen who were not legally qualified as weavers[2]. In order to meet this case,

[1] High rents had been taken as an index of opportunity to raise revenue, when taxation was chiefly levied on the land; and the balance of trade had been regarded as showing favourable conditions of commercial and industrial activity; but both of these were superseded by reckoning the profitableness of investments.

[2] *Growth*, II. 658.

however, the whole system was swept away on the supposition that the capitalist might be trusted to maintain a standard of good workmanship among the men he employed. The experience of a century, and the outcry about technical training at the present time, show that even if the old system of apprenticeship was out of date, the training of workmen could not be wisely left to take care of itself.

(*b*) In the same way the Elizabethan machinery for the authoritative settlement of wages was swept away altogether. The practice of apprenticeship appeared to be so firmly rooted in most trades that it could be argued that there was no need for authoritative backing, but on the other hand the assessment of wages appears to have fallen into disuse and there seemed to be serious practical difficulties in reviving it. The weavers and others insisted on the necessity of taking some action of the sort, but parliament regarded it as impractical and left wages to adjust themselves[1]. The experience of the nineteenth century, and the revival of attempts to fix a sliding scale and to settle disputes between capital and labour, have shown that whatever amendment may have been necessary in the old practice, it was not wise to leave the relations of employer and employed to be a matter

[1] *Growth*, II. 628.

of private bargaining between individuals. Conditions of trade which marked the early nineteenth century, with its sudden fluctuations of demand, and the facilities of supply which were afforded by the introduction of machinery, put the employers in a position of economic strength; so that the standard of life of the workman was in danger of being seriously and permanently lowered[1].

(c) The chief measures which had been taken for the security of the realm were also abandoned. It was held that this was adequately provided for by private enterprise. The Corn laws had directed capital into the improvement of cultivation for the growth of additional supplies of corn; and though the kingdom had ceased to be self-sufficing and imported a considerable amount of food-stuffs, it was still argued that it was politically important to have food grown at home so that there should be at all events a large stock of corn upon which the public could rely, apart altogether from the risks of conveyance by sea. This position was definitely abandoned in 1846 when the Corn laws were abolished and the food supply of the country was treated as a

---

[1] Owing to these conditions the iron law of wages was more nearly true for England then, than it has been either before or since. *Growth*, II. 741

matter of private enterprise ; while similar steps were taken in regard to the mercantile marine by the abolition of the Navigation Acts in 1850.

(37) This new principle of relying on the private capitalist was adopted by many who regarded themselves as keenly interested in the prosperity of the country. They held that *laissez faire* was the best policy for promoting the material progress of this country; and not only so, but that it would sooner or later be recognised by every other country as the best means of promoting its own material prosperity. It was in this way that free play for capital came to be recognised as not only superseding all need for economic regulation within the realm, but as providing the best conditions for the world at large and superseding any attempt to regulate the economic relations between one country and another. This was the doctrine which has been popularised by Cobden; it secured a victory at the repeal of the Corn laws so far as our own country was concerned; and the system of commercial treaties, which was soon afterwards inaugurated, was hailed as a step in securing its general acceptance throughout the world.

This acquiescence in organisation by private capitalists as a satisfactory system had a direct result on thought and discussion in economic subjects. To have them all brought under one simple formula, by the exclusive attention which was now given to private capital, was a simplification of the problems in regard to the resources of the country and the development of commercial relations. The statement of a few laws appeared to give an adequate account of many matters which had hitherto been puzzling through their complexity; and the chaos of political and social affairs was reduced to order by the enunciation of a few principles. There were indeed some doubts expressed even then as to the one-sidedness of the science. It was the Political Economy of private capital, and of hoards of material wealth, and the motive of the capitalist in the use of his money was simply that of getting wealth. There were economists who protested that Economic Science only dealt with one side of life and did not profess to be a guide to duty; but the prejudice against economics as a dismal science was not allayed by such assurances; on the one hand it was denounced as materialistic since it was wholly concerned with the increase of material wealth; and on the other it seemed to render human life merely mechanical and to discuss the play of great economic forces, which operated upon men and which could not be controlled by human beings.

(38)   During the latter half of the nineteenth century it came to be generally admitted that though *laissez faire* had many advantages in regard to the production of material wealth, it was not altogether satisfactory from a social point of view. Capital is a great power; but capitalism, the social system which gave it free scope, was fraught with many evils. In the forties, fifties and sixties legislative enactments which limited the free play of private capital were regarded as mere exceptions; but in the seventies and still more in the eighties, they were generally accepted as beneficial legislation for which no excuse or apology was necessary. Before the end of the century, socialistic enactments of many kinds in regard to internal affairs were carried through in complete disregard of the principles of *laissez faire*. The correctives had been advocated by philanthropists, and though the capitalist was strongly opposed to them and argued that they would do more harm than good, one limitation after another on the power of the capitalist to organise his own business in his own way was carried through.

The roots of modern philanthropy can be traced to the earlier part of the reign of George II[1], in the provision for the sick which was made by the founding of hospitals in so many counties, and the institution of

[1] *Christianity and Politics*, p. 154.

the Royal Humane Society. But the philanthropists, and those who desired to improve the condition of the poor, felt that they could do but little without State backing. Clarkson and Wilberforce brought the power of the State to bear on the merchants who were engaged in shipping slaves to the West Indies[1], and from this time onwards there was a steady progress on the part of the State in the protection of apprentices whether as chimney sweeps or in factories, and in regard to the employment of women in factories, mines and fields. The reconstruction of the Poor Law in 1833 is an indication that the nineteenth century was endeavouring to struggle more effectively against evils for which remedies had been sought in the sixteenth century; and the change of administration, which became uniform throughout the country, seems to have been a very great gain.

The State also took up new functions which had hardly been admitted during the sixteenth or seventeenth century. The advance of medical knowledge rendered it possible to insist on sanitary measures both as regards work and as regards the conditions of housing which would never have been thought of in the olden days; and the State had never regarded itself as responsible for the education of children till it came to co-operate with the pioneers

[1] *Growth*, II. 607.

of education in 1833[1] and organised a system of
national education in 1870 including compulsory
attendance at school.   The Franco-German War so
impressed the English public as to render the country
anxious to follow the German lead, and to see that all
the citizens had obtained at least the elements of
education.   As is often the case, however, with
imitators, the English educational reformers were
not very successful in reproducing the best features
of the system they held up to admiration.   Since 1870
there has been continual discussion in every part of
the country about the relative importance of one
subject or another, and about the advantages of
various methods of instruction; but it seems to be
assumed by all parties that the aim in view is that of
enabling the individual to make the most of his
opportunities and to get on in life.   The aim in
Germany has been entirely different, as it has been a
constant endeavour to train the child to realise his
part in the life of the community and to be fit to
render useful service to the community.   The competition of individuals for honours or for pecuniary
rewards is not nearly so prominent in Germany as it
is in our educational system, which does little to
encourage patriotism or to accentuate the communal
element in personal life.   We have need to remember

[1] *Growth*, II. 750.

that "every disposition of mind, every word, every conception is the result not of an individual, but of a social process. The greatest genius even, thinks and feels as a member of the community; ninety per cent. of what he possesses is a trust conveyed to him by forefathers, teachers, fellowcreatures, to be cherished and conveyed to posterity. The majority of everyday persons are little more than indifferent vessels into which flow the feelings and thoughts of contemporary millions[1]." Religious education may help a child to realise his place in a supernatural kingdom; but it is the communal spirit in the secular sphere that ought to be cultivated, if England is to be saved from the narrow selfishness that arises from concentrating attention on the training of individuals to take part successfully in the struggle for existence.

Besides the action of the State in taking over education and other new functions, there was another force which was still more directly opposed to the claims for unfettered action which were put forward by capitalists. The growth of Trade Unions is the most noticeable feature of the nineteenth century in England. In 1802 they were treated as criminal associations, while in 1904 they had attained such

[1] Schmoller, "The Idea of Justice in Political Economy," in *Annals of the American Academy*, IV. 708 (March 1894).

power and influence that they were able to secure remarkable privileges and were set free from the penalties which had been imposed upon them in disputes in the Civil Courts[1].

Socialist legislation and Trade Union action has gone on increasingly within the realm, although

[1] It does not appear that the immunity which was granted to Trade Unions has been altogether justified. The dangers to the welfare of the community which were anticipated by Sir John Walton (4 *Hansard*, cliv. 1295), have been at least illustrated by the action of the Welsh miners and other strikers during the war. The power of the Trade Unions in securing such a position is very remarkable, and the Trade Union Congress of 1916 showed a disposition to learn to use this power rightly. Trade Unionists from the first have set themselves to improve the standard of life of the labourer; this includes not merely wages, which shall be adequate for his maintenance, but such regularity of employment and conditions of work as shall give him greater status in the community and render him less liable either to sudden disturbances or to long depression. A great improvement has come over the position of the workman in these respects. For many years economists argued that it was impossible to obtain these advantages by combination, while now there are some who allege that the advantages would have come anyhow in the progress of society apart altogether from the action of Trade Unions. Whatever the truth of the matter may be, it is the general belief among the working classes that they never would have improved their bargains with capital if the practice of individual bargaining had been maintained, and that it is only by the collective action of men, who are associated together for this object, that the standard of life has been improved. It is at least something that there should be a general recognition that the standard of life does not depend merely upon the play of mechanical forces, but that it is something which can be raised, and which in many classes of the community ought to be raised.

the principles of *laissez faire* have been strongly maintained in regard to the external relations of the country, but this exception cannot be maintained. The doctrine of *laissez faire* and the principle of free exchange explain the rapid progress which takes place in a community of enterprising men; but it implies that there is a constant struggle between the various elements of which society is composed, a competition of individual with individual, of class with class, and of nation with nation. And this is not an ideal state of affairs. However injurious State interference may have been in the past, by checking individual enterprise, the experience of the nineteenth century has convinced the British public that State interference is sometimes necessary. It is admittedly desirable in matters of hygiene and education; and it is coming into vogue increasingly in connection with industry, since State regulation is the most effective means of preventing either capitalists or associated labourers from pursuing their own interests to the injury of the community. It is, however, much to be regretted that in our time the necessary interference with the individual should appear to be haphazard and arbitrary, instead of depending on a carefully thought out policy as to what is good for the country as a whole, both in its moral and material aspects.

The material interests of the country are a matter of public concern, for apart from other considerations they give us the opportunity of securing the welfare of the inhabitants. Any country which neglects them, sacrifices the opportunity of making the most of her own population, and of doing her best for people within the sphere of her influence.

It can no longer be assumed that the free play of private interests gives us a result which is identical with the public interest; and the material prosperity of the community is a thing which must be safeguarded and fostered. Nor can it any longer be assumed that the industrial rivalry of nations will be kept in check by an increased sentiment of brotherhood, so that each will prosper alike side by side. The nation which is not at pains to develop its own life, on the material side, has little prospect of making progress in welfare at home or in influence on the world.

III. LESSONS FROM EXPERIENCE

(39) At first sight it may seem as if the history
of the past had been a mere flux in which one form of
economic organisation after another had been discredited in turn, and passed away. But this is not the
case; each of the organisations of economic activity,
which we have viewed in turn, has served its purpose
for a time, each has been more effective than that
which it superseded, each has given man a greater
command over the comforts and conveniences of life.
From each we may derive some experience that may
be of use in facing the future. What is most striking,
during this time of war, is the power and effectiveness
of the newly created economic organisation. It has
turned all the activity of the country into one direction
in order to enable the armies and navies, which we have
organised and maintained on an unheard of scale, to
win the victory. To this one national object the
systems of communication both internal and external,
and the industries of the country, have been directed;
never before was there a time when the nation showed
the same energy and success in organising the activities
of the country for one common purpose.

The nation has been able to accomplish this task because of its credit and the consequent command of capital; partly by works carried on as departments of government, and partly by entering into partnership with private capitalists and associations of capitalists, it has succeeded in attaining this result. All that the government could do in the sixteenth and seventeenth centuries was to try to direct private capital into the lines that were beneficial to the public, through the attractions of concessions and bounties; but now it has the means, as it never had before, of undertaking public services itself, and thus turning the energies of the nation into the fields where they are wanted. The experience of last century has shown the possibility of improving the public administrative system. The Royal Council under the Stuarts had no conspicuous success in dealing with the problems of rural, industrial, and commercial life, even on the small scale on which they were presented; but during the nineteenth century, governmental departments and inspection have been developed in such a fashion as to give constant help in regard to improved legislation.

(40) We can also profit by the experience of the nineteenth century in our conception of the aim which the nation should keep in view; the aim of Elizabeth

and the Stuarts was chiefly that of preventing the waste of the resources of the realm, and developing these resources. But the nineteenth century has made us realise that the State is not merely concerned with material resources, but with human beings as well; and that it is possible to aim not merely at preventing the strong from doing injustice to the weak, but at maintaining and improving the standard of life in the poorer classes of the community. The effort has been most successfully made by skilled artisans, though even they have relied upon the assistance of the State; and it is most desirable that the State should turn its attention to the improvement of the standard of life in rural districts. The sixteenth century legislators were greatly concerned about obtaining an increased food supply and improving the practice of agriculture. That is a problem in the present day; but there is also need to attack the questions of the housing of the rural poor and of maintaining them in wholesome conditions of life. There is reason to hope that the improvement of the standard of life in rural districts would check the migration towards the towns, and thus tend to check overcrowding in urban districts and to limit competition for employment among unskilled labourers.

(41)   The importance of raising the standard of life and giving better opportunities to the rural population

is generally admitted. The best means for realising this aim is a question for experts, who are fitted to guard against practical difficulties, and who can estimate the cost of bringing about a real revolution in the condition of the rural labourer. Elizabethan economists recognised that the best means of encouraging tillage lay in making the profit of the plough as good as that of the fleece, and the problem of making the status of the rural labourer, who is a highly skilled man, as good as that of the artisan, seems to a large extent to be a question of money. Unless rural products obtain a remunerative price in the markets, neither the capital sunk in land, nor the capital which gives employment on land, nor the labourers who work the land, can obtain adequate remuneration; it is idle to attempt to improve the condition of any one, merely at the expense of other factors in rural production. Recent attempts to improve the condition of the labourer by allowing him to rent small holdings, have involved him in responsibilities which he is not always able to undertake. Unlike the small holder of the Middle Ages, he does not practise subsistence farming, but farms for a market. There are very few commodities which he has an advantage in marketing as compared with the large producer; he is less able than the large producer to hold his own in bad seasons, and there is a greater risk of his attempting to go on producing crops, while he starves the land and gradually exhausts it. Men of exceptional thriftiness and energy may battle successfully with untoward circumstances; but in order that a class of small holders may be maintained and perpetuated, it is necessary that they should have the reasonable expectation of remunerative prices. There was in the eighties and nineties a large area of land in England which went out of cultivation altogether, while millions of acres are not as productive as they might be[1]. The improvement of agricultural skill has rendered it possible to obtain an average of some thirty or forty bushels per acre steadily, without exhausting the soil, if the land is properly farmed; but it cannot be properly farmed unless the price which is obtainable renders high farming remunerative; and therefore for the full utilisation of the rural resources and the maintenance of the standard of comfort of the rural labourer it is essential that the State should ensure a price of corn which is higher than that which has ruled since the eighties. The competition of the great wheat growing areas in the west of the States, and in Canada, has rendered it impossible to maintain the efficiency which English agriculture had reached in the sixties and seventies. The most

[1] Middleton, *Recent Developments of German Agriculture* [Cd, 8305] p. 6.

hopeful expedient for enabling the agriculturist, whether he has a large estate or a small holding, to obtain the necessary capital for carrying on his work is that facilities should be given which render it possible for him to borrow prudently from the State; and the certainty of obtaining a remunerative price would be the most important element in enabling him to borrow and to do his land justice.

The State is in an advantageous position for realising its aims, both with regard to the development of the material resources of the country and for improving the moral welfare of the people, by the use of its credit. The government of this country has failed to demonstrate that it can organise business better than the individual employer, or that it has greater enterprise than the individual capitalist; but the intervention of the State may be advantageous, not only because it reduces the wastes of competition[1], but because the State by its credit can obtain capital more cheaply than any individual can. The British government has frequently used its credit to obtain capital for unproductive expenditure in war; it is much to be desired that, like other public authorities, it should engage in works of public utility, and in

[1] See my article on the "Progress of Socialism in England," *Contemporary Review*, XXIV. 879.

stimulating peaceful industry as well, by the use of its credit.

State actions of this kind need not supersede individual energy. Private hoarding and accumulation would still go on; they would be essential in order that the public might have money and be able to take up government loans; State borrowing involves the existence of private capitalists, just as taxation involves the existence of individual proprietors. Matters might indeed be managed so that additional enterprise was called forth; and that men who have no capital of their own, might get their chance of showing their capacity. It has sometimes been remarked that the Scottish banks with their system of Cash Credits, have done a great deal to foster the diligence and capacity of young tradesmen in Scotland[1]. There is at present a danger lest the beginners in any industry should be crushed by giant capitalists or great associations[2]. We may learn from Germany how public credit can be employed, so as to stimulate and foster industrial enterprise.

At all events as a lender of capital the State would be able to lay down conditions as to the use made of that capital by landlords and others, and thus to secure very real control over the management of land

[1] *Growth*, II. 454.
[2] Sir B. C. Browne in *Times*, 9 Sept. 1916, pp. 5 and 7.

and the welfare of the rural population. It would have power to enforce that those who, as capitalists, employ labour in rural districts should provide cottages that would suffice for the labour which they set in motion. The State could make the granting of loans conditional on suitable arrangements being made in regard to game. The policy of granting loans on a large scale has already been tried in Ireland; and there seems no good reason why a similar scheme should not be introduced into England also. It might be possible to preserve the local knowledge and personal interest, which is only possible under individual management, with the supervision and control which the State might rightly exercise over the use made of the capital which it had provided.

The introduction of such State-cooperation with private industrial enterprise would appear to tend in favour of a greater measure of stability in business, and the consequent reduction of fluctuations; in so far as this was the case, one great cause of industrial unrest would be removed. It is the speculative element in business, and the large gains which are sometimes made by private individuals at the expense of other individuals, or of the public that rouse the sense of social injustice; exceptional profits in times of national stress are not unnaturally viewed with suspicion. There may be no immunity from labour disputes and strikes in government departments and factories, but owing to the fact that they are public affairs, there is less room for personal jealousy; the extension of the practice would lead to a distinct diminution of the causes of mutual irritation. The exceptional profits and the windfalls made by individuals are most likely to rouse jealousy; and the more State possession of capital introduces regularity into the conditions of employment the less likely are such disturbances to be of frequent occurrence.

(42) In the middle of the nineteenth century the question was raised whether the competition of individual capitalists, which was the normal condition of business in England and America, was spreading so rapidly in other lands that it could be conveniently taken for granted as approximately true for the world as a whole[1]. In the present day this condition has to a great extent ceased to hold good even in England and America. Capital ousted the independent workmen from many industries in the eighteenth century, and since then the small capitalist has been more and more ousted from business, by the competition of great associations and trusts. If these associations are to be controlled, there is need of a national policy

---

[1] *Literary Remains of Richard Jones*, Preface, p. xiv.

which takes account of national interests. An economic science which merely considers individual possessions and the play of individual interests is hardly capable of stating these national interests at all. It is difficult to take account of the security of personal property in the nation, by adding up the importance of which each individual is conscious in the preservation of his personal property. The progress of the nation is sure to be, for a time at least, injurious to certain individuals; and the wealth and capital of the nation is to be reckoned as an important factor in the organisation of economic activity. The nation can do much for the development of its own resources by providing facilities for communication, by making permanent improvements in the land, by planting industry, and by training the population of the country to take their part in its economic life.

It is well that each nation should be free to control such matters in accordance with its own traditions and ambitions, and it is thus important that it should preserve economic independence. Germany is not perhaps to be blamed if she has pursued German interests and consciously exploited other countries for her own advantage[1], but any country is to be

[1] Englishmen certainly have no right to blame her: List pointed out that England had habitually endeavoured to render other peoples subservient to the progress of her

blamed which consciously submits to accept such a condition of economic dependence and tamely consents to sacrifice its own future development. This principle, which was neglected in the eighteenth century, is now generally adopted in the British Empire; each of the overseas dominions is now regarded as responsible for its own development, and is free from any duty of remaining economically dependent upon the Mother Country.

(43) Freedom for economic development is, however, not inconsistent with the recognition of the advantages which may arise from international cooperation. Countries differ in climate and soil and in the nature of their productions. There are some which have special advantages, there are others which can supplement the special disabilities and defects of their neighbours. It is desirable that so far as possible countries should consciously co-operate for each others' good. Where the political connection is permanent, as between Great Britain and the various parts of the Empire, such conscious co-operation may be devised without serious difficulty; and the Allies, through temporary emergencies, have been brought together to see that conscious co-operation

industry and that in adopting Free Trade there was no change of policy in this respect. *National System of Political Economy* (ed. Nicholson), pp. 33, 70.

in meeting the special wants induced by the special conditions of war, may be most advisable; the growth of such economic co-operation, consciously aimed at and pursued, will be more stable and lasting than the haphazard intercourse, with its incidents of glutted markets and occasional interruptions, which arise when international commerce is left entirely to be conducted by private capitalists.

(44) Indefinite progress in the improvement of social conditions lies within our reach, if we will only be in earnest about developing the Body Economic in every part of the Empire, and encourage the co-operation of economic activities, while being ready to respect the efforts of every other country to foster its economic life. So long as we are careful to make the most of our own resources, material and personal, the prosperity of our neighbours need rouse no suspicion or jealousy; but the alleged friendship of our industrial rivals can never be an adequate reason for letting things drift, by neglecting our own resources and by being content to leave our economic activities unorganised. There is always another step forward which can be taken in putting down injurious conditions at home or in the countries under our influence; and for such gradual improvement we have command of sufficient knowledge and of a

most powerful agency for bringing it into effect. In
the old days a well managed household could only
deal with a limited area, and side by side with it
there might exist centres of tyranny and misrule.
The burgesses of the city could only take a narrow
view of prosperity and were suspicious of opulent
men and jealous of other cities; through national
organisation we have the means of dealing with the
country as a whole; while there is the opportunity of
devolving power on various local authorities, in those
cases where knowledge of local detail is essential to
good administration. There has besides been an
enormous increase of knowledge as to the causes of
physical evils, such as ill health; we speak with
surprise of the indifference of the eighteenth century,
but it must be remembered that ignorance as to the
possibility of finding a remedy for many of the
admitted evils of the human lot, was one excuse for
the failure to make the attempt. The State has now
the power to improve material conditions in many
ways, and by legislative enactment and improved
administration can put down admitted evils in the
conditions of work and the conditions of life.

We may see our way to indefinite progress on the
material side; but it is important to remember that
social welfare depends, not merely on the externals
of life, but on human character as well; so long

as we look only at external phenomena we get little help in seeing how to bring about an improvement in human beings themselves. There are sentimentalists who believe that by playing on material conditions they can build up improved sentiments; as in the eighteenth century many Englishmen believed that by forcing the colonists into a position of economic dependence they could foster the sentiment of loyalty towards the Mother Country. Similarly it has been hoped that mere contact and opportunities of frequent intercourse would break down racial jealousies and induce a feeling of human brotherhood; but this opinion has not been justified by experience, either in Ireland or in India. There are other social philosophers who hold that men are entirely guided by conscious interest, and that the consciousness of common interest affords the basis on which social peace may be established; but the fact that capital and labour engaged in industry have interests in common has not sufficed to bring them into perfect accord. It is not by looking at the phenomena of human life in the past and fixing on one factor alone that we can initiate progress in human life itself. There is need to recognise the limitations of experience in order to get beyond it[1], and to set forth

---

[1] Compare Nicholson, *Principles*, III. 426.

ideals which have not been given in the experiences of the past, but which we may hope to realise in the future.

Ideals for the life of the individual man arise when he comes to be conscious that he has a share in a larger life than his own. The ideal of being a worthy citizen of a great State, and of fitting himself to take a part in the work of that State, is one which has inspired many patriots in the past, and may be most effective, not only in the special emergencies of war, but in the conduct of civil affairs as well. It can have a certain definiteness and concreteness, because the great States of the world have left material records of their achievements, which appeal to the imagination; but if we would secure some inspiration that is universal in place and time, and applies to all ages and to all peoples, we must pass beyond the limitations of the kingdoms of this world and their conflicting interests and jealousies. It is only in religion, and in the acknowledgement of an overruling God to whom every man is responsible, that we find the condition which is most favourable to the creation of a federation of the world.

BOOKS AND PAPERS ON ECONOMICAL
AND SOCIAL SUBJECTS

"Mr Spencer's Sociology," in *Theological Review*, XIV. 334. (July 1877.)

"The Progress of Socialism in England," in *Contemporary Review*, XXXIV. 245. (January 1879.)

The Growth of English Industry and Commerce. Cr. 8vo. pp. xiv + 492. Cambridge University Press, 1882.

"Letters from India," in *Cambridge Review*, 8 February, 15 February, 22 February, 1 March, 8 March, 15 March, 1882.

"English Industry and Commerce," a Reply to Prof. Thorold Rogers's critique of the *Growth of English Industry and Commerce*, in *Academy*, 27 May, 1882.

"On the true statement of the Malthusian Principle," in *Macmillan's Magazine*, XLIX. 81 (December 1883), and reprinted in the *Path Towards Knowledge* (1891).

Christian Opinion on Usury with special reference to England. Cr. 8vo. pp. x + 84. Macmillan and Co., 1884.

Politics and Economics, an Essay on the nature of the Principles of Political Economy together with a survey of recent legislation. Cr. 8vo. pp. xvi + 275. Kegan Paul, Trench and Co., 1885.

The Alternative to Socialism in England, a Paper read to the Cambridge Economic Club, 1885, and privately printed.

Editor of the *Report of the Proceedings of the Industrial Remuneration Conference* (January 1885).

"The Rise and Decay of the English Yeomanry," in *Church Quarterly Review*, XX. 286. (July 1885.)

"The Repression of the Woollen Manufacture in Ireland,"
  in *English Historical Review*, I. 286.   (April 1886.)
"Temperance Legislation," in *Contemporary Review*, L.
  647.   (November 1886.)
*Political Economy treated as an Empirical Science; a
  Syllabus of Lectures*.   Macmillan and Bowes, 1887.
"City Opinion on Banking in the XIVth, XVth, XVIth
  and XVIIth Centuries," in the *Journal of the Institute
  of Bankers*, Vol. VIII. pt. II. p. 53.   (February 1887.)
"Positivism, its truth, and its fallacies," a Paper read at
  the Manchester Church Congress, October 1888, and
  reprinted in the *Path Towards Knowledge*, 1891.
"The Commercial Policy of Edward III," in *Royal
  Historical Society Transactions*, N.S. IV. 19.   (1889.)
Craft Guilds, a Paper read before the Society for the
  Protection of Ancient Buildings, 1890.
*The Growth of English Industry and Commerce during the
  Early and Middle Ages*.   8vo.   Cambridge Uni-
  versity Press, 1890, and subsequent editions, 1896,
  1905, 1910.
"What did our Forefathers mean by Rent?" in *Lippin-
  cott's Magazine*, p. 278.   (February 1890.)
"The Ethics of Money Investment," a Paper read before
  the London Ethical Society, *Economic Review*, I. 13.
  (January 1891.)   •
"Progress of Economic Doctrine in England in XVIIIth
  Century," in *Economic Journal*, I. 73.   (March 1891.)
Review of Gross's *Gild Merchant*, in *Economic Journal*,
  I. 222.   (March 1891.)
*The Path towards Knowledge, Discourses on some diffi-
  culties of this day*.   Cr. 8vo. pp. vii + 241.   Methuen
  and Co., 1891.
The Use and Abuse of Money.   Cr. 8vo. pp. xxiv + 219.
  John Murray, 1891.
Nationalism and Cosmopolitanism in Economics.   Presi-
  dential Address to Section F, British Association,
  Cardiff, 1891.

"A Plea for Pure Theory," in *Economic Review*, II. 25. (January 1892.)

"The Relativity of Economic Doctrine," in *Economic Journal*, II. (March 1892.)

"Perversion of Economic History," in *Economic Journal*, II. 491. (September 1892.)

"The Perversion of Economic History," a Reply to Prof. Marshall, *Pall Mall Gazette*, 29 September, 1892, and *Academy*, 1 October, 1892.

The Growth of English Industry and Commerce in Modern Times. 8vo. Cambridge University Press, 1892, and subsequent editions in 1903, 1907.

"Die Regelung des Lehrlingswesen durch das Gewohn-heitsrecht von London," in *Z. f. Social- und Wirth-schaftsgeschichte*, I. 61. (1893.)

"On the laws of the Mercers' Company, Lichfield," in *Trans. of Royal Hist. Society*, N.S. VII. 109. (1893.)

"Political Economy and Practical Life," in *International Journal of Ethics*, III. 183. (January 1893.)

Review of the *Discourse of the Common weal of this realm*, by E. Lamond, in *Economic Journal*, III. 669. (December 1893.)

"Economists as Mischief Makers," in *Economic Review*, IV. 1. (January 1894.)

"A Living Wage," in *Contemporary Review*, LXV. 16. (January 1894.)

"Wages," in *Lombard Street in Lent*, 1894.

"Dr Cunningham and his Critics," in *Economic Journal*, V. 508. (September 1894.)

"Why had Roscher so little influence in England?" in *Annals of American Academy of Political and Social Sciences*, V. 317 (November 1894), and translated in the *Jahrbuch für Gesetzgebung, Verwaltung und Volkswirthschaft im Deutschen Reich*, XIX. 383. (1895.)

With Dr E. A. McArthur, *Outlines of English Industrial*

History. Cr. 8vo. pp. xii + 274. Cambridge University Press, 1895, and subsequent editions in 1898, 1904, 1910, 1913.

"The Gild Merchant at Shrewsbury," in *Royal Hist. Soc. Trans.,* N.S. IX. 99. (1895.)

"Walter of Henley," in *Royal Hist. Soc. Trans.,* N.S. IX. 215. (1895.)

Strikes, Publications of Church Social Union, Series B. 4. Boston, Mass., 1895.

"The General Election—Prospects of Social Legislation," in *Economic Review,* v. 501. (October 1895.)

Modern Civilisation in some of its Economic Aspects, pp. xvi + 227. Methuen and Co., 1896.

"The Corrupt Following of Hippodamus of Miletus at Cambridge," in *Proc. of Camb. Antiq. Soc.,* N.S. III. 421. (17 November 1897.)

Alien Immigrants to England. Cr. 8vo. pp. xxiii + 286. Swan Sonnenschein and Co., 1897.

An Essay on Western Civilisation in its Economic Aspects (Ancient Times). Cr. 8vo. pp. xii + 220. Cambridge University Press, 1898, and subsequent editions in 1902, 1911.

"A Plea for the Study of Economic History," in *Economic Review,* IX. 67. (January 1898.)

"English Imperialism," in *Atlantic Monthly,* LXXXIV. (July 1899.)

"The Value of Money," in *Quarterly Journal of Economics,* XIII. 397. (July 1899.)

"The Good Government of an Empire," in *Atlantic Monthly,* LXXXIV. (November 1899.)

An Essay on Western Civilisation in its Economic Aspects (Mediaeval and Modern Times). Cr. 8vo. pp. xii + 300. Cambridge University Press, 1900.

"American Currency Difficulties in XVIIIth Century," in *Economic Review,* XI. 10. (January 1901.)

"The Teaching of Economic History," in *Cambridge Essays on the Teaching of History,* 1901.

Report of Committee of Lower House of Convocation on Clerical Poverty and Clerical Charities (No. 369). (April 1902.)

"The Imperialism of Cromwell," in *Macmillan's Magazine*, LXXXVII. 72. November 1902, and reprinted in *The Wisdom of the Wise*, 1906.

"Economic Change," in *Cambridge Modern History*, I. 493. (1902.)

Preface to *Cambridge Gild Records* by Mary Bateson. Cambridge Antiquarian Society, 8vo. Publications, No. XXXIX., 1903.

"Back to Adam Smith," a Paper read to the Scottish Society of Economists, December 1903, reprinted in *The Rise and Decline of the Free Trade Movement*, 1905.

"The Failure of Free Traders to Realise their Ideal," in *Economic Review*, XIV. 39. (January 1904.)

"The real Richard Cobden," an Address to the Compatriots Club, June 1904, printed in *The Rise and Decline of the Free Trade Movement*, 1905.

The Rise and Decline of the Free Trade Movement. Post 8vo, pp. 168. Cambridge University Press, 1904, and also 1905.

"Tariff Reform and Political Morality," in *Compatriot Club Lectures*, 1905.

"Letters from South Africa," in *Cambridge Daily News* (28 August, 4, 11, 25 September), 1905.

Unconscious Assumptions in Economics. Presidential Address to Section F, British Association, Cape Town, 1905.

"Impressions of South Africa," in *National Review*, XLVIII. 228. (April 1906.)

"The Wisdom of the Wise," *Three Lectures on Free Trade Imperialism.* Post 8vo. pp. 125. Cambridge University Press, 1906.

"The Ordinary Degree at Cambridge," in *Oxford and Cambridge Review*, I. 115. (June 1907.)

"Back to the Land," in *Economic Review*, XVII. 389. (October 1907.)

"Impartiality in History," in *Revista di Scienza*, I. 121. (Bologna 1907.)

"Early Writings on Politics and Economics," in *The Cambridge History of English Literature*, IV. 295. (1909.)

"Economic History of Cambridge," in *Ely Diocesan Remembrancer*. (February 1909.)

Christianity and Socialism, a Paper read before the Victoria Institute. (February 1, 1909.)

The Moral Witness of the Church on the Investment and Use of Wealth, an Open Letter to the Archbishop of Canterbury. Cambridge University Press, 1909.

"The Problem as to the changes in the course of the Cam since Roman Times," in Cambridge Antiquarian Society's *Communications*, XIV. 75. (1909.)

"Is it possible for a Free Trader to be a good Citizen?" in *Irish Church Quarterly*, III. 47. (January 1910.)

Christianity and Social Questions. Cr. 8vo. pp. xi + 232. Duckworth and Co., 1910.

The Case against Free Trade, with a Preface by the Right Hon. Joseph Chamberlain. Cr. 8vo. pp. xvi + 137. John Murray, 1910 and 1914.

Socialism and Christianity, together with a Paper read at the Church Congress. S.P.C.K. 1910.

"Francis Bacon and the Office of History," Presidential Address in *Royal Hist. Soc. Trans.* 3rd Ser. IV. (1910.)

Article on "Free Trade" in the *Encyclopaedia Britannica*. Cambridge University Press, 1910.

Preface to *The Strength of England*, by J. W. Welsford, 1910.

"National Institutions in England and in Scotland," Presidential Address in *Royal Hist. Soc. Trans.* 3rd Ser. V. (1911.)

"Letters from Palestine," in *Cambridge Daily News*. (March 20 and 21 and April 1, 5, and 8, 1911.)

"Feudalism in England and Scotland," Presidential Address, *Royal Hist. Soc. Trans.* 3rd Ser. VI. (1912.)

The Causes of Labour Unrest and the Remedies for it. A Memorandum prepared for the Moral Witness Committee of the Convocation of the Province of Canterbury. John Murray, 1912.

"The Economic Basis of Universal Peace—Cosmopolitan or International?" in *Economic Review*, XXIII. 7. (January 1913.)

"The Guildry and Trade Incorporations in Scottish Towns," Presidential Address in *Royal Hist. Soc. Trans.* 3rd Ser. VII. (1913.)

"Architectural Design," in *Royal Hist. Soc. Trans.* 3rd Ser. VII. 16. (1913.)

"The Organisation of the Masons' Craft in England," in *Proceedings of British Academy*, VI. (1913.)

"Ulster under Personal Monarchy," in *The Covenanter*, p. 2. (24 June 1914.)

"The Appeal to Force," in *The Covenanter*, p. 18. (24 June 1914.)

Christianity and Economic Science. Cr. 8vo. pp. viii + 111. John Murray, 1914.

Report of Committee of Lower House of Convocation of Province of Canterbury, on Dilapidations. No. 490. (April 1915.)

"Economic Problems after the War," in Prof. Kirkaldy's *Credit, Industry and the War*, 1915.

"Differences of Economic Development in England and Scotland," in *Scottish Historical Review*, XIII. 168. (January 1916.)

"Cambridgeshire Materials for the History of Agriculture," in *Proceedings of the Cambridge Antiquarian Society*. (January 1916.)

Christianity and Politics. 8vo, pp. 263. John Murray, 1916.

English Influence on the United States. Cr. 8vo. pp. xii + 168. Cambridge University Press, 1916.

INDEX

Printed in the United States
By Bookmasters